DATE DUE

NO 16 '98			
DC 24 00			
NO 17 01			
DE 13 04			
SE 3 0 09			

DEMCO 38-296

ARCHITECTURAL
RENDERING

ARCHITECTURAL RENDERING

PHILIP CROWE

⊥⊤

STUDIO
VISTA

STUDIO VISTA

an imprint of

Cassell
Villiers House, 41/47 Strand
London WC2N 5JE

British Library Cataloguing in Publication Data
A catalogue record for this book is available from
the British Library.

ISBN 0-289-80074-9

This book was designed and produced by
Quarto Publishing plc
6 Blundell Street
London N7 9BH

Editor: Judy Martin
Designer: Pete Laws
Project coordinator: Laura Sandelson

Typeset in Great Britain by
Typestyles (London) Ltd, Essex.
Manufactured in Hong Kong by
Regent Publishing Services Ltd.
Printed in Hong Kong by
Leefung-Asco Printers Ltd.

CONTENTS

Preface 6

The Practice of Architectural Rendering 8

Rendering: The Art of Communication 10

Content and Composition 18

Materials and Techniques 40

Step-by-Step Guide 84
Projects in Progress

Portfolio 148

An International Catalogue of
Architectural Renderings

Preface

Among the many features that contribute to the timely value of this book is a unique portfolio section containing examples of the architectural illustrator's craft from around the world – drawings and paintings that until recently have seldom been seen outside their countries of origin, much less compiled for comparative evaluation as they are here. The initial instructional sections present the processes and techniques by which perspectivists create their specialized illustrations. The rich, varied results of such methods, as successfully applied by professionals, comprise the greater part of the book's gallery of images. They offer an unusual opportunity to study the cultural and aesthetic influences, differences and similarities which exist within and between each nation. The perspectivists themselves, for the most part, have been practitioners for many years and have achieved some distinction in their own professional communities.

In addition to the richness of representation, the most remarkable aspect of this volume is its international scope. The phenomenon of the illustrator's re-emergence as both a gifted interpreter of non-built architecture and as an independent, legitimate professional can no longer be overlooked or merely acknowledged as an ancillary field to architecture. This collective emergence owes much to the recent activities of three representative organizations – the Society of Architectural and Industrial Illustrators (SAI) in Britain, the Japan Architectural Renderers' Association (JARA) based in Tokyo, and the American Society of Architectural Perspectivists (ASAP) in the USA.

Given my own intimate involvement as one of the three founders of the American Society of Architectural Perspectivists, it has been my privilege to observe the increasing interest in the work of architectural illustrators worldwide, an interest not limited to design professionals, as might be expected, but encompassing an ever-widening sector of the public. The circumstances that have brought this about are not easily identified: suffice it to say that the skilful artistry of perspectivists has generated an excitement not hitherto seen on this scale.

Within the expanding network of previously unassociated individual practitioners in America, and certainly among the more serious illustrators elsewhere, a special camaraderie has developed. Given the relative isolation of the majority of freelance illustrators, any organization that allows for stimulating professional, social and intellectual interaction fulfils a much-needed function. As with any group of like-minded individuals, the intensity of interest among perspectivists about their field of activity is one of the key guarantors of any organization's success. The American Society of Architectural Perspectivists and its fellow societies have played a central role in focusing an impulse for association that has been quite remarkable.

Two principal reasons for the strength of this impulse have been an unaddressed need for a professional affiliate body and a healthy inclination to demonstrate an unusual skill. Most perspectivists seldom have the opportunity to know, let alone meet, anyone else in their field. Even less frequently is their work displayed for professional or public review. Through its annual competition and exhibition, *Architecture in Perspective,* ASAP has created the means for celebration of an accomplished artform and of its highly skilled practitioners. Similarly, the SAI and JARA provide a forum in their respective countries for discussion and promotion of the profession, for the encouragement of excellence and an appreciation of the finer points of illustration for their own sake.

This interaction is but one aspect of an ongoing mutual pursuit of excellence. In addition to the brief exposure to originals that occasional exhibitions permit, most practitioners and aspirants must rely on books to assuage a nearly insatiable desire for reference information with which to study more deeply the lessons of distinguished examples. Recent publications, although excellent resources in themselves, hardly seem sufficient to appease the growing educational need for illustrators (who are mostly self-taught), nor adequate to demonstrate current activity in a very vital field.

Every artist constantly strives to better his or her technique or explore a new one. With communication between practising professionals easier than ever before, the opportunities to do so have increased tremendously. It is generally the case that today's architectural illustrators have acquired their skills through some initial combination of private study and academic training, and from subsequent practice and experience. It is also generally acknowledged by even the most celebrated professionals that an aesthetic mastery of the discipline as demonstrated by its finest exponents requires a most serious commitment to the work of drawing. It is towards that rarefied level of skill, exceeding the parameters of a practised competency, that contemporary illustrators aspire. There is clear evidence of their efforts and achievements in pursuing that goal to be seen in the many contributions to this volume.

Through the cooperation of perspectivists worldwide, *Architectural Rendering* effectively realizes a representative international view of this specialized field of illustration. I expect that the book will become an invaluable reference work to instruct and inspire the professional, the student and the drawing enthusiast about a time-honoured subject once again coming into its own.

Frank M. Costantino, ASAP, FSAI, JARA
Co-Founder
President Emeritus
Secretary
The American Society of Architectural
Perspectivists

THE PRACTICE OF ARCHITECTURAL RENDERING

RENDERING:
THE ART OF COMMUNICATION

CONTENT AND COMPOSITION

MATERIALS AND TECHNIQUES

RENDERING:
THE ART OF COMMUNICATION

The world of ideas revealed in this book should astonish you. These are visions of the future; for the illustrations presented here show a wealth of projects which at the time of their preparation were still unrealized dreams in the minds of their designers and those who were eventually to commission them. Some of these exciting projects may not yet have been built. Indeed, some may never see the light of day, but the majority can now be seen in their intended settings.

Many of the project designers will themselves have prepared illustrations of their projects, but by far the greater number will have been produced by professional illustrators — renderers, perspectivists, delineators, call them what you will — whose business it is to interpret the designers' intentions. Many outstanding illustrators work entirely on their own, others are part of studio teams, producing collaborative artwork. This use of the word 'artwork' should not be misinterpreted. Perspectivists are concerned with the strictly utilitarian task of representing concrete proposals for building structures in landscape or townscape settings, which imposes imaginative constraints that are compensated by the acquisition of exceptional technical ability. They are not artists but craftsmen and women highly skilled in visual communication. Why and how they choose to communicate in this way is the subject of this book.

Initial design concepts

The building design process is a complicated series of interactions, and the process by which designers visualize their designs in the early stages has been the subject of some study. Not only does the designer have to explore the potential of particular design concepts to his or her own satisfaction, he or she also has to communicate these concepts to the design team. The results are 'esquisses' or design sketches, which may be quite freely drawn, with little detail. This is the simplest form of rendering, often carried out with whatever materials are to hand.

This development sketch of a competition-winning project in Japan, by a London architect, is typical of the rapid exploration of design ideas prepared by in-house design teams. The massing of the project and its relationship with adjoining buildings are indicated with great economy of means in the elegant pen drawing.

This exciting rendering, airbrushed in gouache and acrylic, of a project in Melbourne, Australia, presents the design dramatically. The brilliant cladding of the tower is silhouetted against an impossibly blue sky, yet is firmly rooted in reality at its base. Many of the design details have not been completely finalized, but the concept is clear and forms a striking image, made all the more convincing by the photomontage technique.

In this project for a European executive car manufacturer, the design ideas are worked up in marker pen to show elements of the landscaping, the building form and its cladding, which consists of panels of transparent and opaque glass. The visual information is presented in enough detail to ensure that the client is both interested and informed.

These can then be worked up into a more finished form, enabling the designer to evaluate the ideas, make modifications and produce a final design concept which can then be communicated to the client. As this process is such an intimate one, it is rare for it to be subcontracted outside the design team. Brilliant designers who are not very skilled at three-dimensional representation may produce very crude illustrations of their intentions, but these can serve the immediate purpose admirably. Of course, there are some few designers who are also first-class illustrators, in which case you can be sure that what is in the designer's mind and what eventually happens on the ground will exactly correspond.

The role of the illustrator

When the design concept is finalized and approved in principle, the illustrator starts to play a major role in the communication process. For now the client, the one who is making the investment, must be persuaded that the designer's ideas will succeed in

This is a competition entry for a Japanese city centre site. The main subject is illustrated in some detail, set off by the surrounding buildings shown in simplified form. The coloured support is an ideal basis for the night-time scene, perfectly integrated with the opaque body colour of the gouache artwork to form an exciting, but not extravagant, image which will impress the competition assessors. Note the use of vertical perspective, with a vanishing point below the picture.

visual and practical terms. The client may be an individual, a trust fund, a board of directors, a government department, or a panel of competition assessors. When the client is satisfied that the design solution solves the problems posed, approaches can be made to other bodies for funding and investment decisions, planning and development approvals. There may be consultation exercises involving public meetings and exhibition of the proposals. Eventually campaigns may be launched for selling or letting the project, requiring visual material for brochures and press releases.

The input of the architectural illustrator is vital for the success of every stage of this realization process. To the illustrator falls the onerous task of communicating the designer's thoughts in an easily assimilable form. It is seldom sufficient to rely on written explanations or plans and elevations, which may contain technicalities not widely understood. In a world almost universally conditioned by superb magazine, television and video presentation, it is the three-dimensionally realized visual image that has the most persuasive force.

This being the case, why not take the unusual step of looking upon the profession of architectural illustration as being part of the advertising industry, where skills of visualization are used to 'sell', in this context to ensure acceptance of, a particular building project? Remember that a first-class illustration can act as a powerful persuader.

The target audience

Decision-making bodies can be composed of experts who are fully aware of the technical criteria upon which a submission should be judged. They can also be composed of lay people, with no knowledge of the 'isms' of current architectural taste, but who may have an intuitive appreciation of the way in which a projected development might affect their local community, provided the proposal is presented in a form they can understand.

For the former, the presentation might be a theoretical one, showing

Two different but equally successful brochure pictures show how a rendering can indicate the impact of a major development in broad landscape (top) or close detail of an individual building (above). They arouse the reader's interest, so that he or she turns the brochure pages to discover more about the practical details of the project.

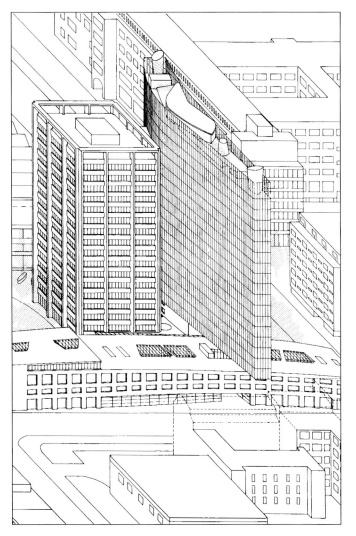

An unambiguous ink line technique (right) leaves nothing to the imagination. No figures or vehicles distract from the straightforwardly explanatory, almost diagrammatic nature of the rendering.

The shopping precinct (below) forms a mere backdrop to human activity, although its architectural detail is accurately rendered. The client requested that human interest should be paramount, as it was important to convince the local community of the project's suitability.

the reasoning behind the design in abstract terms, or an absolutely accurate, clinical representation of the project, allowing no possible misinterpretation of the designer's intentions. The latter group may be interested less in the technical or stylistic expertise of the designer than in the way the project interacts with its surroundings. For them humanity, not statistics, is all-important, and a perspective featuring local colour can be an instant success. An illustration showing people going about their daily lives with the building as background makes the point that the project is to serve the community, and not the other way around.

Taking a brief

You may be asked to take your instructions directly from the project designer, or your briefing may include a meeting with the commissioning client to discuss his requirements on the form and presentation of the rendering. Bear in mind that your client may have a preference for a particular style of illustration. Ideally, you will be able to show previous work; an alternative option is to take examples of the work of other illustrators whose styles approximate to your own. You must make sure that there are no unresolved problems here before you start work.

Defining your task

A problem that you may encounter is the representation of a poorly designed project. Architectural masterpieces are thin on the ground and the chances are that the bulk of your work will be reflecting mediocrity or worse. The obvious solution is to reject commissions of this kind, but very few illustrators are so highly thought of that they can afford such an elitist attitude.

Decisions on a project can be made subconsciously within seconds of viewing an illustration, so a bold, decisive image can be of great significance. The dramatic sky, deep shadows and robust gouache technique make a strong impact here, with the arrangement of figures leading the eye to the main subject, a small office building.

The answer is to adopt a detached view, regarding the task as a purely mechanical exercise that has to be performed to the best of your ability. But make no mistake, no amount of technical bravura will produce a fine illustration from an inferior subject.

You should also consider the vexed question of 'artist's licence'. How faithfully must your illustration represent the intentions of the designer? Should you draw figures larger than life, so that the apparent bulk of the building is reduced? Should you relieve the blankness of a flank wall by planting large trees, which in practice would have no room to grow? Should unfortunate design features be obscured by passing vehicles? Should buildings be given ample settings by placing them further apart than they would be in fact?

All these minor deceits encourage the viewer to be more receptive to the project than would otherwise be the case. We all know that the advertising profession is adept at performing such sleights of hand, which in many cases are more sins of omission than outright untruths. But in the sphere of washing powders and coffee blends, the consumer is conditioned to expect distortions of the truth. In the world of architectural illustration, however, truth is of the utmost importance because the end product that results from the communication process of which you are such an important part is so uncomfortably permanent. So don't cheat, your reputation is at stake — perhaps we should not think of ourselves as being in the world of advertising after all, but stick to our role in the communications business.

Presentation

We have now reached the stage when the end-use and general form of your illustration have been determined. How can it best be presented?

If you are not to make use of your original artwork, remember that any form of reproduction is an influence that may not be beneficial. Very fine line work, or delicate watercolour, coloured pencil or pastel techniques may not reproduce well, either in print or as a transparency. If your work is to appear in brochure form, or will be projected at a meeting, make sure that your original is bold enough to make a strong statement. Large format overhead projection transparencies often give sharper results than the more usual 35mm slides, unless these are back projected, but it is unlikely that you

This magnificent large-scale rendering of New York's Park Avenue would be an ideal subject for a presentation exploring the image with a video camera. The detail is so fine and of such consistent quality that any number of sequences would be possible. The combined techniques of airbrushing and coloured pencil drawing produce an image of almost photographic realism.

will have any control over the quality of the projection equipment, so allow for the worst case.

For display purposes, do not forget the new generation of photocopiers, laser copiers and bubble-jet copiers, which can produce excellent large-format results within minutes. Where large monitor screens are available, complete audio-visual presentations using one or two perspectives can be outstandingly effective. If the original work is sufficiently large, the video camera can move around the surface very much as it could do on an architectural model, exploring the illustration from a distance and in close-up. This has the advantage over the computer walk-through simulation, in that an immense amount of incidental detail can be shown on the artwork which it is not practical to programme into a computer within the time-scales and budgets generally available.

The method of reproduction or display can be discussed with your client at your briefing, when you can decide upon the scale and medium for the work as well as its style. Often, the matter of presentation consists only of mounting, possibly framing, the artwork and then despatching it to grace some boardroom wall, never to be seen again; so make sure you have it photographed first to include it in your own records.

DE CE TERRIBLE
PAYSAGE,
TEL QUE JAMAIS
MORTEL N'EN VIT
BAUDELAIRE

FROM
T·H·E C·I·T·Y

Theoretical studies like this (left) bring together idealized building forms, in this case drawn from the past, often with an implied message. This is an intriguing exercise in compositional depth.

Immaculately airbrushed on canvas, this painting (above) manipulates building reflections in a way that the casual passerby would never see in reality. Startling patterns of light and form make the spectator look at buildings, and images of them, in a new way.

Alternative forms of architectural rendering

So far we have been concerned with the commercial applications of architectural rendering. Many illustrators are not commercially minded at all. Designers and theorists have always produced visualizations of their ideal concepts to promote their philosophical arguments, and they are in the fortunate position of being able to allow their imaginations free rein.

Often they lead architectural fashion through the publication of their drawings in the professional press, but it has to be said that on occasion these can be so abstruse as to negate the purpose of illustration, which should be one of immediate communication.

Other draftsmen are seduced by their chosen medium, spending days on masterpieces often not tied to any particular project. Finally there are artists who find architectural subjects of interest, reflecting aspects of architecture that engage the viewer in a painterly way. Often using photographs as a base, they examine existing buildings, or invent new building forms, drawing on their imaginations

They all enjoy a freedom which is denied to the perspectivist by the strict terms of reference that apply to this field of illustration — the obligation to represent facts as they are or will be.

CONTENT AND COMPOSITION

This rough concept sketch in fine-line marker indicates the character and massing of the proposed buildings, with rapid figure drawing to give scale and interest. This is the riverside entrance to a landscape festival site. From sketches like this the design was developed in detail.

Before putting pencil to paper, you must draw on your experience to advise your client on any factors that may affect the commission. The first, and most crucial, of these is the purpose of the illustration. For a press release in a local newspaper, for example, a fairly bold and simple monochrome treatment might be the most appropriate, as fine detail would probably be lost in the printing. For a high-quality colour magazine or brochure, a full-colour, detailed treatment might be needed, but with a tight publishing deadline you might not be able to produce artwork to the standard required within the time available. A presentation to a committee would probably demand a large rendering, mounted and possibly framed, with additional colour copies supplied for individual members, adding time and extra costs to the commission. Clients usually have a budget to work to, and as you gain experience you will be able to forecast with some accuracy the costs of alternative techniques and illustration sizes, based on the area of the illustration and the time needed to produce it.

Content and technique

You must establish clearly the type and amount of information to be conveyed and relate this to the

techniques at your disposal. The requirements can range from a rough concept sketch showing the mass of a building and its relationship to its surroundings, to an impressionistic view that suggests modelling, surface finishes and landscape proposals, as an aid to the designer while the project is being developed. The commission may be taken further when design details have been finalized, requiring a photo-realist illustration taking many hours.

This more developed impression in broad and fine markers includes just enough detail to show the colours of materials, the elevational treatment, and the importance of the landscape.

At this stage, you should ask further questions of the client that enable you to decide how you should approach the commission. Is all the information to be shown necessary for the end-use of the illustration? Is all the information available at the current briefing, and is any of the detail likely to change? If changes may be requested, you need to give careful consideration to the technique you will use for the finished artwork — marker and watercolour renderings, for example, are notoriously difficult to alter.

Design detail

One aspect of commercial rendering rarely discussed is the illustrator's unpaid design input. Particularly in sketch or preliminary proposals, when design details have not been finalized, you may be asked to fill in design detail from your own experience to provide a convincing illustration. This implies either that the client or commissioning agent is looking for cost savings, or that the commission has been put out too early in the design process. Some artists take such a brief as a compliment to their knowledge and skill; others may regard it as an imposition and decide to reject the commission unless there is a suitable increase in the fee.

Identifying the viewpoint

Once the major decisions have been reached on the subject matter and the medium for the illustration, a suitable viewpoint has to be determined. You may find there are conflicting views within a client organization on the best viewpoint to be adopted. One person may want the rendering to focus on the imposing main entrance, another on the number of lettable floors, while the landscape treatment and context

The precision possible with watercolour is exploited to the full in the superrealist effect applied to this rendering of an office development. The superb image is low-key, but interest is generated by the attention to minute detail. Every subsidiary element, whether vehicles, figures or landscaping, is effectively placed to make a positive contribution to the composition.

of the site may be more important to to others. You should try to resolve such conflicting requirements so that your briefing concludes with clear instructions.

In addition to the direction of the view, the distance must also be considered — the closer the viewpoint, the greater the amount of detail that can be included. For large-scale projects, the viewpoint will obviously have to be some distance away if the whole scheme is to be shown, but an important corollary to this is that definition and texture may be lost and colours severely modified.

Above: The landscaped setting of this museum building in Frankfurt was of great significance; both elements are beautifully captured in coloured pencil.

Focusing on the main entrance of an office block, this delicate watercolour incorporates the fine detail of the exterior and the intricacies of the interior lobby.

Elements of the composition

Once you have established the approximate viewpoint, you can start to think about the composition and its dramatic effect. At this point you have to tread warily. Your reputation for accuracy may suffer if the building is distorted in your attempt to produce an eye-catching presentation. Skilful composition can emphasize those elements that the client feels are important without resorting to exaggeration. Highly dramatic effects are not necessarily wrong, but the practical purpose of the illustration must always be borne in mind.

Certain principles of composition can be applied that lead to the viewer becoming more involved with the illustration. They derive from the axiom that the picture should never be divided into equal halves, by vertical, horizontal or diagonal lines or features. If this happens, the eye cannot rest; it moves from side to side of the dividing element, and the immediate impact of the illustration is considerably lessened. If you have to adopt a more or less symmetrical division of the picture plane, you

Above: The dramatic clouds and dark shoreline planting throw this coastal project in Japan into sharp relief. This dynamic approach, with the cloud forms cleverly composed to complement the mass of the buildings, is highly appropriate for this large, heavily modelled complex with its rocket-like towers hinting at other worlds. The technique and subject are perfectly combined.

need to use compositional devices that direct the eye back to the principal subject.

Perspective lines can direct the eye into the middle ground of the picture, and if the edges are less detailed, or 'bled off', this tendency is reinforced. You can similarly focus attention on the central area by framing the edges of the picture with tonally dark elements seen in close up, in contrast to more sparing detail applied to the main subject. Dark ground tones or angled ground shadows, even false ones, also draw the viewer into the image.

Additional features such as people or vehicles, that are incorporated to give scale to the composition and tie the building into its setting, should be used in a positive way. In an illustration of, for instance, a retail development project or transport interchange, they may be as important as the building itself in conveying a necessary illusion of reality. A successful composition ensures that the viewer's eye concentrates on the point of the illustration.

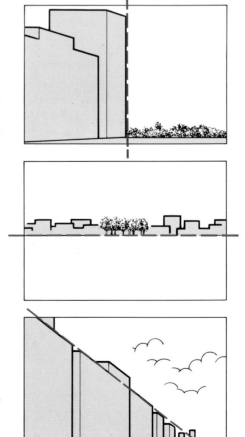

Symmetrical divisions present visual problems that need correction. In this vertically split composition (top left) the weight is left of centre; a strong sky and ground level interest on the far right would assist the balance. Equal horizontal division (centre) does not correspond to real experience; when looking at the horizon we register far more sky than land. A strong diagonal (below) overweights the lefthand side of the composition and directs the eye out of the picture at the bottom right.

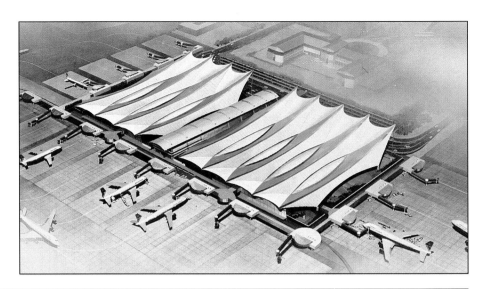

A competition entry for design of an airport terminal, rendered with gouache and aerosol sprays, shows how cloud effects can be used to subdue less important detail.

This superb panorama of Washington D.C. produced to illustrate several development sites, shows the complexity inherent in large-scale aerial views. An immense amount of detail is included, drawn in coloured pencil and white acrylic, at the specific request of the client.

VIEWPOINTS

In perspective renderings of exteriors, viewpoints fall broadly into three categories: aerial; gound-level, meaning the view from normal eye-level; and subterranean, or mole's eye views. Interior viewpoints pose special problems, discussed on pages 32-33.

Aerial viewpoints

These range from an angular view, as if the building is seen from an adjoining high-rise block, to the high-altitude panorama of a large-scale development. Whatever the amount of new detail required, you will almost certainly be faced with the problem of including areas of surrounding landscape. This can be particularly time-consuming in illustrating urban areas, where the extent of existing buildings to be shown can easily equal or exceed that of the main project. If you are not supplied with aerial photographs from the same viewpoint, a great amount of time has to be spent setting up positions and heights of existing features (see page 27). These also have to be handled in such a way that they do not visually overpower the main subject matter. In line work, representing detail at a distance can be very time-consuming. There is no alternative to practising the gradual elimination of detail over distance, but masking out and lightly overspraying the background, or spraying mist or cloud forms through which the

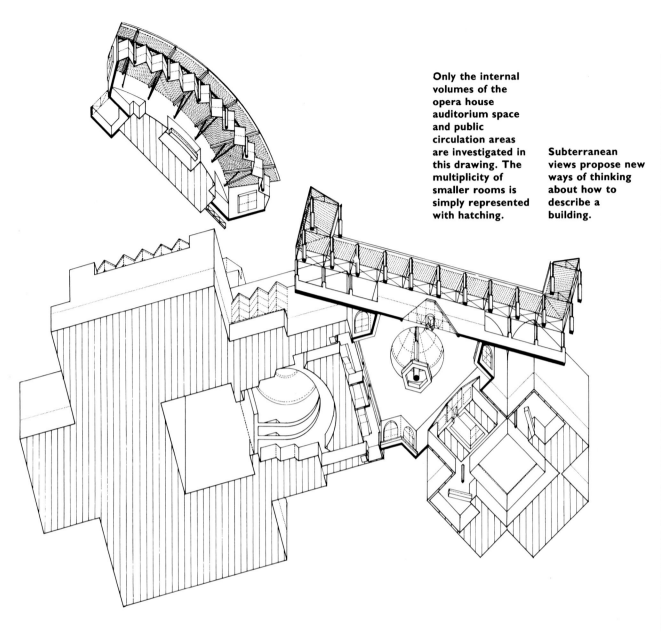

Only the internal volumes of the opera house auditorium space and public circulation areas are investigated in this drawing. The multiplicity of smaller rooms is simply represented with hatching.

Subterranean views propose new ways of thinking about how to describe a building.

subject can be seen, are both useful ways of cutting down on the amount of non-relevant background material, which then only needs to be hinted at briefly.

Ground-level viewpoint

This reflects the most likely experience of the average passer-by, representing the view from an ordinary eye level. A possible variation is the pavement-level view, which gives dramatic impact; this cannot be faulted on grounds of accuracy, but may be rejected on grounds of improbability. A single view, in any case, may not be enough, bearing in mind that the normal angle of vision is approximately 50°. For the largest projects, you may have to adopt a

wide-angle approach, but take care that you do not allow significant distortion to occur.

One solution is to move the viewpoint further away so that the project falls within the normal viewing angle, but in many cases, particularly with urban sites, this viewpoint is impossible to achieve in practice. This problem can arise even with modest developments in narrow streets, where only sharply angled views are possible. The client then has to decide, in the light of his or her requirements, whether to commission a fantasy view or a realistic one. The former option certainly has no value in illustrating the environmental impact of a new proposal. The best solution for a large project, whether on a

congested or an open site, is to illustrate it with a series of views, possibly in sequence, much as the user might experience it.

Subterranean viewpoint

This viewpoint is uncommon, and is more likely to be found as an axonometric construction than as a perspective illustration. It is, of course, totally artificial, but can be helpful when describing the three-dimensional modelling of a facade, as it shows the complete elevation from actual ground level; the normal upward view of a building as seen from close to would leave out the lower part of the elevation. The subterranean viewpoint can be combined with an upward view of the ground floor interior spaces.

This exterior view uses a single vanishing point in the centre of the picture. The radiating perspective lines focus on the subject. All the planes facing the viewer are at right angles to the line of vision, leading to distortion at the bottom corners. The illustrator has overcome this by clever use of foreground planting.

SETTING UP

Before you start thinking about setting up your perspective, you must be able to read complex design drawings. Persuade your client to give you only those drawings that are strictly relevant, so that you are not swamped with paper; you can always ask later for clarification of points on which you are uncertain.

Perspectives fall into two broad categories — single point and multiple point. There are innumerable textbooks that explain the mechanics of setting up perspectives, so here we will concentrate on one or two aspects that typically cause difficulties.

Single-point perspective

In this system there is a central vanishing point contained within the boundaries of the illustration. Single-point perspectives are used for interiors and enclosed spaces such as courtyards and streets; curved streets may have more than one vanishing point, but the principle remains. The planes of the structure that face the oserver are shown at right angles to the line of vision,

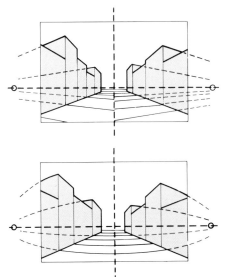

with the flanking planes receding into the distance in the centre of the picture. The viewer is thought of as being within the enclosed space.

The major problem is one of distortion at the edges of the picture, brought about by the artificial nature of the construction — in reality, the eye cannot focus in this manner. A minor problem is produced by the fact that all the lines at right angles to the line of vision are horizontal, and not in true perspective. A modified form of

To avoid corner distortion here, the planes facing the viewer are shown in perspective. This leads to problems with the paving lines in the centre of the picture. The solution is to show the planes facing the viewer as being curved, an unconventional interpretation that, although correct, may not be visually acceptable, simply because it is unfamiliar.

If the single-point vanishing point is taken off-centre and the drawing is faded out in the areas nearest the viewer, at **X**, the problems of corner distortion are minimized.

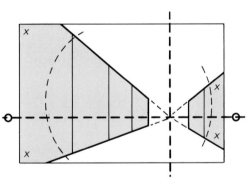

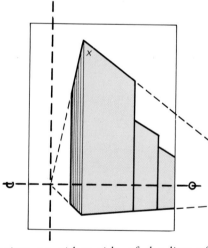

This is the simplest of multiple-point perspectives, using only two vanishing points. If the viewpoint is too close to the building, distortion occurs at the highest point (**X**).

single-point perspective shows the planes at right angles to the line of vision in perspective, but this can be unsatisfactory where horizontal lines — paving or ceiling joints, for example — cross the line of vision, forming an angle. In reality these lines would form a continuous curve which might look out of place in the conventional illustration, simply because we are not used to seeing it.

The difficulties can be eliminated to some degree if you take a viewpoint that is off-centre, and fade out the areas nearest to the viewer, which would be technically out of focus.

Multiple-point perspectives
Most perspectives are multiple-point, where all planes lead to vanishing points on either side of the line of vision. Again, two problems occur. The first is that if the viewpoint is too close, only the areas immediately above and below the horizon line — the viewer's eye level — can be shown with reasonable accuracy. Distortion increases with height until the resulting image becomes quite unacceptable. A dramatic mole's eye view makes matters even worse. The position can be corrected to some degree if you create vanishing points for the verticals above the image area, but this is not always acceptable because it is not the way the mechanism in the brain

In this typical view of a low-rise building, using only two vanishing points, the viewpoint is taken far enough away to eliminate distortion. If the spectator point had been closer, or the building higher, the illustrator would have encountered problems.

interprets the messages from the eye when we look at a real building. Nonetheless, vertical recession can be very effective and can have an unusual impact simply because it makes us think again about what we expect to see.

The second problem is that of representing a long building viewed frontally. From a close viewpoint, it would be impossible for the eye to take in the whole facade in one movement. If the conventional viewpoints are used, distortion occurs at that part of the building closest to the viewer. As in single-point perspective, curves are the only solution, with the maximum height of the building shown directly opposite the spectator point. With this approach, the only straight line will be the horizon line, all other horizontal lines being subtly curved. Much more work is required to produce such an illustration, but it is accurate. It is also useful for very wide-angle panoramic views.

It would be logical to carry this principle of curvature through to the vertical lines, but this is not recommended. Taken to its ultimate extreme, it produces a 'fish-eye'

effect, which is very time-consuming to produce and is limited in application.

Distortion in aerial views

Aerial views, particularly close-ups, suffer from the same distortional problems. They are in effect mole's eye views in reverse, creating acute proportional difficulties in the foreground. Solutions are to move the viewpoint further away, eliminate the foreground completely, or adopt the

Vertical recession can be used to good effect in close-up views, where the use of a vanishing point above the image reduces distortion and incidentally provides a dramatic composition.

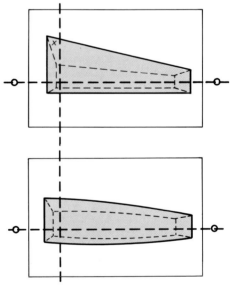

A direct view toward the end of a long facade produces distortion opposite the viewpoint at X (above centre). One way of correcting this is to use the principle of curved horizontals to achieve correct proportions (above). In the main illustration (top) only the horizon line is horizontal. All the lines above and below it are curved. This clearly indicates the limitations of the conventional perspective method.

curved perspective principles already discussed. Convergence of verticals, to a vanishing point below the image rather than above it, can be of help.

At least with an aerial perspective there is no limit to the distance from which you can view the subject, as there is with a ground-level view. This can eliminate the vertical convergence factor. Imagine an aerial photograph of a building taken from so far away that all the verticals do actually appear vertical in the photographic image. If you zoom into the subject, they remain vertical, but the area shown in the picture is much reduced and the subject appears flattened. This foreshortening effect is very useful for large, difficult subjects.

Much time can be saved by 'eyeballing' aerial views, without the complex setting up of the usual ground-level perspective. To do this, you first grid the plan area, numbering it along two adjacent sides for reference, then prepare a perspective overlay grid, similarly numbered. This grid can be quite large, so that you can move it about until the most suitable angle of view is obtained, and it can be used for other projects, so it is worthwhile making it reasonably

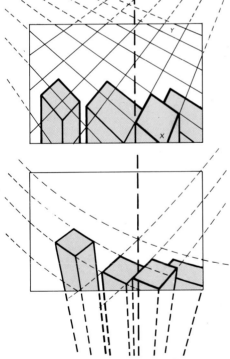

Aerial perspectives can involve acute distortion in the foreground if the viewpoint is too close, as shown at X. It becomes progressively less as you move upwards towards Y. If a vanishing point is taken below the image (above), and the principles of curved perspective are adopted, these problems can be virtually eliminated.

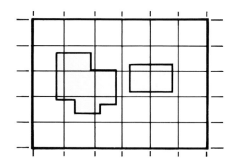

accurate. You then plot the plan over the perspective grid, establishing a simple height gauge in the foreground derived proportionally from one of the side divisions of the grid. Remember that height differences viewed from above can be very slight, and the steeper the angle of view, the less apparent they are. It is very easy to indicate buildings higher than they should be — a useful check is to compare the proportions of height to length.

The use of grids in aerial perspectives can save time. Draw a suitable scaled grid over **the plan of the project (left), with references along the periphery.**

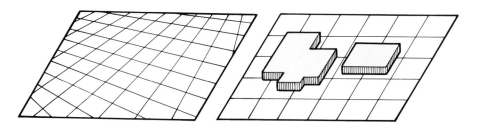

Alternative methods

For any perspective rendering, grids can be a great time-saver. You can prepare them yourself or obtain printed grids. There are also patented

Select a pre-drawn perspective grid large enough to cover the area you need, at the desired angle of **view (above left). Using the selected portion of the perspective grid, key the grid lines as on the original** **plan grid, plot the plan coordinates and draw it out. Establish a height scale in the foreground and** **draw up the project in three-dimensions (above right).**

USING A FACADE MODEL

Building a facade model is very easy. Using only those design elevations likely to be visible from your preferred viewpoint, mount them on card, cut them roughly to shape, and tape them together. You can either draw out your perspective or use an instant photograph, enlarged on a photocopier.

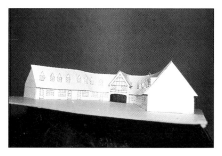

A simple card model using the front and side elevations of the building assists the artist in visualizing the overall impression of the curved construction from the required viewpoint, and in locating the architectural detail.

drafting aids available for perspective drawing, some of doubtful value. But whatever system you use, the days are long gone of setting up a perspective for which the vanishing points might be halfway across the studio floor. You can draw preliminary drafts to a very small scale, so that the vanishing points are contained within the drawing board area, then enlarge the drawing on a photocopier, possibly in sections pasted together, and trace it down at the required size.

For those who find even limited setting up too difficult or time-consuming, one solution is to build a facade model, using the design drawings cut out and pasted onto card, positioned so that the main elements of the building can be seen from the selected viewpoint — you do not have to produce a complete model. Photograph the model, make a tracing from the print, then enlarge the tracing to the size you require.

Another useful method is to draw directly from the model using a sheet of acetate held in a simple card mount, rather like a site sketch. Again you can enlarge this on a photocopier to provide the basis of your rendering. As you can move around the model before you start to draw, you can select the best viewpoint without having to prepare alternative drafts.

When you have produced the perspective draft, or alternative versions, obtain formal approval of this stage from your client before proceeding with the final version. Keep your preliminary drafts for some time — they can be useful reference if the artwork has to be expanded or altered later.

Setting up by computer

By far the easiest way to set up a complex perspective is by computer. Most design offices can prepare outline plots of their proposals, which can be used as a basis for finished artwork. Innumerable views can be generated, so that the client can select the viewpoint before you take the illustration further. It is unlikely that there will be arguments over accuracy — although computers are not

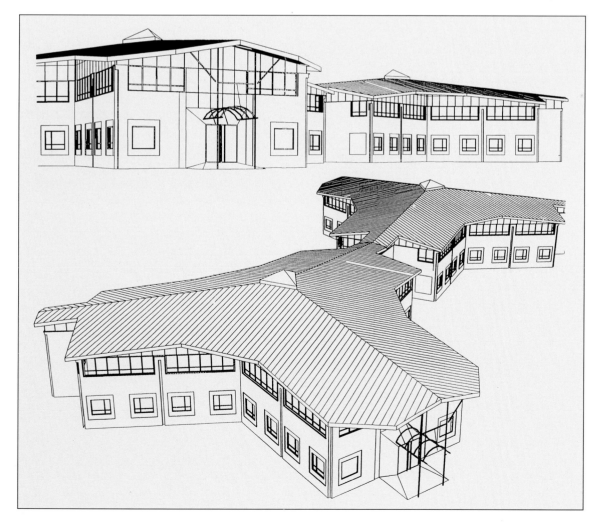

Once basic design information is fed into a computer, there is no difficulty in generating as many alternative viewpoints as you need for final selection. These line plots can then be enlarged or reduced on a photocopier to form the basis of your finished artwork.

Photomontage techniques are ideal for showing the impact of new developments on existing sites. If you take care in the initial photography and plotting stages, particularly on green-field sites, there is no reason to doubt the accuracy of your illustration. In this case two identical prints were made, the montage was painted directly on one of them and rephotographed. It should be quite difficult to detect the new work in the final print.

infallible — and you will be making the client responsible for clarifying the brief unambiguously .

If you know that your client has computer facilities, you should ask for provision of computer plots to be part of your contract.

Photomontage

You might consider this as an appropriate technique when a highly accurate and convincing image is required. When using a photographic image as the artwork base, you need to know the camera viewpoint, height and angle of lens vision at whatever format and aperture you are using. This is particularly important for open views when the project you are

illustrating cannot be directly related to existing structures. Large-scale maps enable you to plot the camera and subject positions and derive site sections so that you can relate the respective heights. You need a spirit level on the camera if a flat horizon is not visible, and a compass for checking sight angles.

There are computer techniques that can scan existing photographs in relation to ground plans and plot the positions of new structures, but whereas these are fairly common for civil engineering applications, they are generally too costly for individual building projects. Simple graphic techniques, working out angles on plan and section, are accurate for most

purposes. When you are dealing with a built-up area, you can easily determine heights and vanishing points by reference to those of adjoining buildings.

You can paste down the finished perspective in the appropriate position on a base print, or insert it as a 'mosaic', making sure that the paper thicknesses are the same. Alternatively, you can paint the rendering directly on the base print using an opaque medium. Whatever your method, take care to blend the new work with the old, not only in the use of colour and tonal values but also in the amount of detail shown. Most media dry matt, so work on a base print with a matt or semi-matt surface,

In using photomontage techniques in a built-up urban context, it is quite easy to relate the details of the new project to those of adjoining property, as this will already have been surveyed as part of the design process. Vanishing points can be interpolated from those on the base photograph.

In close-up photomontage work, take care to indicate colour, texture and detail compatible with the existing surroundings. If this is done at a sufficiently large scale, your fine detail will blend in when the artwork is reduced.

otherwise the montage elements stand out when the work is rephotographed. If you encounter this problem, try spraying the surface of the montage with matt fixative to produce a uniform surface finish.

Accuracy in rendering

While accuracy is important, it need not be taken to extremes. The client expects you to make an accurate impression of the position and bulk of the building, the colour and texture of the materials, and details of adjoining structures, roads and landscape. The precise subdivisions of window frames or the cast of shadows may be less important. You will learn by experience how to be selective.

The illustrator can face difficulties in defining interior spaces, particularly if the surfaces are of uniform tone or colour. In this case the linear features are helpful in indicating the three-dimensional structure of the interior.

INTERIORS

Interior views are usually of a single space and are frequently one-point perspectives. They present the familiar problems of distortion, particularly evident in high volumes of short depth. The best answer may be to frankly acknowledge the artificial convention of the illustration, remove the front wall of the space and place the viewpoint outside it. If you are looking down the length of a directional space, such as a shopping arcade, the use of a single-point perspective is almost inevitable; but a two-point perspective looking into the internal angle of an interior volume gives more convincing spatial results. Whatever system you use, try not to take in too wide an angle of vision.

Here the renderer has successfully used the artificial lighting scheme to indicate the nature of the space.

Describing interior space

The quality of lighting in an interior often causes a problem – how can you differentiate between surfaces with no sunlight and shadow to help you? The artificial lighting scheme may be of significant design importance. In large spaces such as concourses or office floors, there may be a deliberate attempt to provide uniformly even lighting; the effect of this in a rendering is to make the whole space appear visually flat and uninteresting. In such cases you may have to rely solely on structural or decorative linear features – columns, skirtings, dados and cornices – to define the forms. You may even be forced to introduce a fictional lateral light source, if it is important to depict the junctions of wall and ceiling planes.

Large public spaces probably have few textured surfaces to give definition, so the lines of wall cladding, floor tile or ceiling patterns can be used to create an impression of volume. Domestic interiors may confront you with the opposite problem, since they are typically more 'busy', with textured wall finishes, hanging fabrics and carpet patterns which are all to be represented in diminishing scale.

Interior detail

The greatest clues to the size and characteristics of a space can be the relative sizes of the furnishings and the occupants. Here we come up against the greatest difficulty of all for the perspectivist. Whereas we generally view the exterior of buildings in a transient manner, when driving or walking past them or entering a building, we appreciate the interior in a far more intimate and intensive way. We have plenty of time

This magnificent cutaway rendering is full of detail which it would have been impossible to include in one illustration in any other way. Meticulous planning is necessary to ensure that all the important elements are indicated without confusion. This illustration is both a diagram and an architectural rendering, and it requires exceptional skill to combine these aspects successfully.

to look around and examine the detail of the space, and the illustration of an interior needs to reflect this more comprehensive interest.

You must be able to indicate detail and texture at close quarters, without taking so long that you run out of time. You will often be asked to supply all the incidental detail yourself, unless the client is an interior designer. Only the positions of furniture and fittings may be established, with a general indication of their types, colours and surface finishes.

You must also have a good grasp of figure drawing. The occupants of the space must of course be shown in natural poses − nothing is more likely to kill an immaculate interior illustration than unrealistic figure drawing. An interior without figures often looks sterile and uninviting, but if you cannot draw them convincingly, it is better to leave them out.

Cutaway views

One room is only part of a sequence of spaces, both within the building and without. A sight of the outside world through a window or a glimpse into the next room through a half-open door help in the game of illusion.

The cutaway interior, or sectional perspective, takes this principle a

stage further. A cutaway looks at the interior spaces from below, from above or from the side, and takes the whole building as the subject, showing the interrelationships of the interior spaces rather than the detailed design of individual rooms. Sometimes a cutaway is made diagrammatic, showing circulation patterns or service runs. Illustration of a multi-storey structure has to be carefully planned if clarity is to be maintained. Main structural elements are often 'ghosted' over the illustration, usually by airbrushing, to tie the interior together, a technique familiar from explanatory illustrations of cars or aircraft.

The indication of furniture and fittings detail at close quarters can be very time consuming, but it is essential for fully finished interior illustrations. The patterns and textures are beautifully brought out in this example.

This watercolour rendering shows a fine balance between the overpowering mountain range and the intricate details of the building project. Too heavy a treatment of the landscape could so easily have overwhelmed the main subject.

LANDSCAPE

The composition of a landscape background is just as important as the composition of your main subject. Your decision on where to locate the horizon line on the paper is critical. A useful guideline is that the horizon should be about one-third of the total height of the illustration, but this may not make a suitable compositional balance if your subject is a very tall structure. You may, in fact, wish to emphasize the vast expanse of an open situation by establishing a low horizon with a huge area of sky. In a high-level view the horizon might come almost at the top of the illustration, but if it has a hard edge it may create an imbalance; in this case it is better to fade out the background.

If you block in the building and the main landscape features on overlays, you can move them up and down your illustration sheet until you find the correct balance. Keep in mind that it is the architectural subject that is the point of the rendering, not its surroundings; for example, if you are

dealing with a mountain location, make sure that the massive background does not overwhelm the composition.

In urban areas, your landscape may consist entirely of built forms, and how much of the existing surroundings you include will probably depend on your client. Unless contextual considerations are important — in areas of great historical value, for instance — you will find that you must concentrate on your client's project and include a minimal amount of adjacent property. This can be rendered in modified tones, or with less detail. As with aerial urban views, indicating a large amount of extraneous detail can take up much of your programme time, so make sure you allow for the level of definition required.

Atmosphere and climate
In most cases your building will be seen against the sky. Think about the purpose of your illustration — is it to excite, shock or simply inform? — before you embark on an elaborate

skyscape. Dramatic cloud formations are acceptable, but they must be as carefully composed as the ground elements. If you cannot find the time to sketch from nature, manuals on cloud recognition are useful.

Aircraft vapour trails, sometimes disappearing behind clouds, distant rain patterns, or shafts of sunlight are all linear devices that can support the composition and give added depth to the illustration. Frivolities such as kites and hot-air balloons are usually an unwelcome distraction!

Your illustration should reflect the local climatic conditions. Temperate latitudes usually have a mixture of open sky and clouds; sub-tropical and high-altitude locations typically enjoy a deep blue, cloudless sky; desert locations and industrial areas often have a high-level dust haze; the tropics often have exceptionally high humidity and the sky is veiled with light-diffusing water particles. Intense sunlight can bleach out colours and upwardly reflected light has a profound effect on shade and shadow intensity. If your commission is in an

Intense activity at ground level is perfectly complemented by a highly dramatic sky, carefully composed to silhouette the main building elements. The whole impression is one of movement and excitement, for which the fluidity of watercolur is ideally suited.

The slow build-up of detail in coloured pencil drawing enables the illustrator to control precisely the final effect. This serene drawing perfectly captures the early morning light and luminous shadows of a North American dawn. Careful observation and good reference material are essential if you are to achieve such convincing results.

area unfamiliar to you, it is always worth checking on the significant climatic factors.

Light and colour

Natural daylight, which is the general setting for architectural perspectives, is composed of direct sunlight and reflected skylight. Sunlight gives life to your illustration, highlighting surfaces and casting shadows that help to give an illusion of form and texture. By contrast, skylight is diffused, and the time of day, season, latitude and climatic conditions affect the relationship between the two.

Background elements are affected by a scattering of light in the shorter wavelengths caused by atmospheric particles, giving rise to the phenomenon of 'aerial perspective'. Distant ranges of hills and forests appear blue, and brighter objects — low clouds on the horizon, for example — appear redder. In very dry climates with a still atmosphere this phenomenon may not be present, and distant features can appear unnaturally sharp and close. This

A surface composed of jointed material takes on a colour which is an amalgam of the main material and its jointing. This is known as colour assimilation. The greater the distance from the viewer, the more the two colours blend. Many joints are lighter in colour than the main material, although conventionally they may be drawn with dark lines. The correct assessment of these variables, as in this illustration, only comes with experience.

could interfere with your main subject, so it may be better to modify the effect. In any case, do not labour background detail — objects seen from a distance simply appear as patches of colour detached from their true forms.

Colour assimilation occurs when the perceived local colour of, say, brickwork or stonework is modified by the joint colour, a mixing intensified by distance. Determining the effect of this process is one of the most difficult tasks for the architectural illustrator.

The observed colour of your building and of its immediate surroundings depends on the spectral colour properties of each material. The light falling on textured or matt surfaces reflects colour diffusely; smooth surfaces reflect colour directly. This is why gloss-painted or smooth plastic surfaces appear stronger than 'eggshell' or matt ones, even though they are the same colour. Damp conditions, when surfaces become coated with a film of

Representing water presents a whole series of problems, in balancing water colour, the surface texture, and reflections from the sky and immediate surroundings. Good references and observation in the field are essential.

moisture, produce the same effect. A surface that reflects light directly appears lighter, or may even lose any distinct colour value. Watch for the changes from sunlit colours to colours in shade — yellows are particularly tricky in this context.

Water surfaces can appear multi-coloured — they are certainly far from

being uniformly blue! Naturally occurring water is often green, yellow-green or yellow-brown, depending upon its purity and the reflections from its banks. Decorative landscape pools have their own colours. Some still areas reflect the sky or adjoining buildings, while parts of the surface caught by the breeze can be very dark,

Representation of distant landscape, particularly from the air, is an artform in itself. Note how in this finely detailed rendering, not only are the tree forms convincingly portrayed, but the actual land formation is shown with great clarity.

The play of light on foreground vegetation repays careful study. This sunlit detail incorporates a wide range of greens and browns. The use of dilute gouache over a fixative gives the broken colour effect.

because what we see are the sloping sides of the ripples with their multiplicity of interrelated reflections.

Landscaping with plants

A major component of landscape is the vegetation. In the distance, ground cover loses its texture, hedges and clumps of trees appear as flat planes of increasingly pale colour, ranging from bluish-green to reddish-blue in the far distance. Foreground planting is a different matter. Sunlight falling on leaves reflects at different angles, producing a host of colours from almost white to the densest, most saturated greens, which under certain lighting conditions may appear almost black.

Some light may filter through the leaves, creating pale greens and yellows. Ground shadows are not cast as solid areas but are broken up by elliptical patches of light. Tree branches and trunks, often thought of as being dark, may catch the light and stand out against dark foliage, particularly if they are lichen-covered.

This illustration depicts young tree growth with a light leaf canopy, to avoid obscuring the building behind. The viewer can take into account that in ten years' time the picture will be quite different.

The trees here are shown in a fuller, more mature form, but building detail at ground level was not considered of outstanding significance. Although the trees play a small part in the whole composition, they are rendered with as much care as the building itself.

Some have a naturally reflective quality, like the bark of the birch tree.

A familiar problem is how to show tree planting without obscuring your client's building. The most common solution is to show short-term tree growth with a much-reduced leaf canopy, but this requires a sound knowledge of the tree's structure, as it will be clearly visible. If you are using known tree species, you must be able to describe them accurately. However you do this, make sure that they do not appear to be stiff, lifeless forms, and pay careful attention to the grouping and composition. A judicious adjustment of tree positions may be in order, to reveal a particular design point in the building, but do not overdo such amendments — it may be that the landscape design is not quite what it should be.

Convincing representation of plantings seen at close quarters can be very time-consuming, but do not fall into the trap of using a loose, sketchy technique for the landscaping when you have gone to some trouble to illustrate the building in full detail. Inconsistency in your approach will not produce satisfactory results — always consider how each element contributes to the whole illustration.

REFERENCE SOURCES

A comprehensive source of reference material is essential, particularly if your drawing skills are limited. Good reference guarantees accuracy and speeds up the drawing process. There are innumerable publications and transfer sheet systems that illustrate stereotyped figures, for example; these inevitably fail to provide precisely the image you are looking for, and if you use them often, your figure drawing will acquire a familiar look that a regular client may notice, to the detriment of your reputation for individuality. It is far better to accumulate a collection of magazine illustrations showing people in a variety of real-life situations. File them under suitable headings — Leisure, Office, Children, and so on — so that you can easily find useful reference for

A stock of up-to-date reference material is invaluable. Traced off or projected, items can be enlarged, reduced or reversed, and modified to suit the image context. Make sure that they form a composition which makes a positive contribution to your illustration, whether they are figures, vehicles or other technical elements.

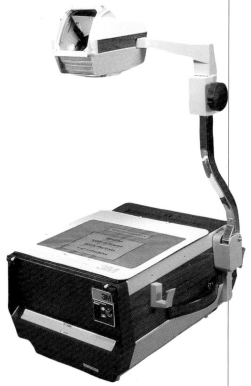

An overhead visualizer that projects hard copy or transparencies onto your work surface can be wall-mounted to take up the minimum amount of studio space. An alternative would be a copyscanner, on which you trace off an image projected from below.

a particular job. Do the same with pictures of cars, commercial vehicles, ships, aircraft and any other technical subjects that you might need. For a specific project, you may need to consult specialist books and magazines related to your subject. Keep your reference files up to date so that they represent the latest fashions and vehicle models.

Your reference material can be traced down with or without use of a light table. It can be enlarged or reduced on a photocopier or visualizer. A cabinet-type visualizer projects hard copy from below, ready for tracing off, and can be combined with a copy camera. The overhead type of visualizer, which is more flexible, projects the reference from above onto your work surface, eliminating the need to make an intermediate tracing; it can take transparencies as well as hard copy. It is not difficult to devise an overhead rig to hold a small single-slide projector. You can use a slide viewer with a large, flat screen to project site photographs, which you can then trace for your landscape detailing.

A projected image or a tracing enables you to move the visual elements around until you establish a satisfactory composition. Make sure when you use different sources of reference that each element appears at the correct scale and perspective in your drawing for the final artwork.

MATERIALS AND TECHNIQUES

You have a wide range of different media at your disposal for both monochrome and colour work. The choice of medium depends not only on the eventual use of the illustration, but also on its suitability for the subject matter. A project featuring large areas of steel or plastic panelling is a candidate for airbrushing with watercolour or ink, a technique ideally suited to representing hard, reflective surfaces. Broad markers are a possible alternative if the illustration is large scale, but neither of these options is suitable for rendering small-scale detail.

Highly textured materials, such as brick or stone, are probably best handled with an opaque medium like body colour or pastel, which enable you to create a varied range of surface qualities, but watercolour on a heavily textured ground can be equally effective if the texture of the support can be used to express the texture of the material you are representing.

A building with a large expanse of glass, or in a broad landscape setting, might benefit from the translucent quality of watercolours, when the white background of the support can be put to good use in creating luminous effects. Line and wash, or markers, would be suitable for a rapid sketch of a design in the early stages of development when gouache, with its solid colour implying decision and permanence, would not.

Many of the different media can be used together to great advantage. Mixed media are fully acceptable if they make a positive contribution to the interpretation of the subject matter, but should not be used merely

The careful application of translucent multiple washes emphasizes the smooth mirror-like quality of this reflective glass facade. The identical vehicles in the foreground cleverly reinforce this image. Notice how the illustrator uses the texture and whiteness of the support to good effect.

In this rendering of proposals for Expo 92 in Seville, the illustrator has successfully combined pen and ink, airbrushing, watercolour, felt marker, tempera and coloured pencil in a brilliant mixed-media illustration. Each medium and technique is carefully chosen for its particular characteristics.

as an eye-catching device. Techniques range from airbrushing large colour areas in watercolour and hand-rendering detail in gouache or ink, to collage, for instance, incorporating coloured papers and photographs, transfer tones and drawn elements.

Delivery times can affect the choice of medium. Highly detailed ink line drawings are very time-consuming, because the technique involves gradually building up the image with innumerable individual marks. A pencil drawing with finely graded tones can be similarly laborious. A graded watercolour wash can be applied quickly, whereas a large area of tempera has to be handled very carefully. One reason why oil paints are rarely used for commissioned illustrations is that they take so long to dry, impractical when there are tight deadlines to be met.

SUPPORTS

Virtually any sheet material can be used as the basis of your illustration, from the wide range of proprietary papers and boards to acetate sheet, or even brown wrapping paper. The medium you intend to use influences the choice of support and whatever you select, the choice should be logical. This means that you will need to give consideration to the colour, surface texture and weight of the material in relation to your medium and working method.

Always choose a colour and texture that brings out the best in the medium. A white or light buff ground is complimentary to watercolour or ink line; a dark tinted paper might be appropriate for pastel, the dark ground emphasizing the brilliance of the flakes of pigment. A free charcoal

sketch takes best on a textured or 'toothed' surface; the grain of the paper also affects the surface quality of a pencil drawing. For line work, particularly when using technical pens, or for hard-edged superrealist images, you need a very smooth surface that gives precise definition. Beware of display board that appears to have a very smooth surface but which causes an ink line to spread and make erasure impossible.

Make sure that the weight of the ground is heavy enough for the medium chosen. Lightweight papers may buckle under colour washes — some papers are available pre-bonded to a backing board, so the task of stretching paper to take washes is eliminated. If you need to use masking, check that the paper will not tear or the surface pull when masking tape or film is removed. Scratching out

A rendering need not have a conventional rectangular frame. In this 'Festival Market' scene the borders are broken at significant points to increase the impact of the illustration in a positive way.

on the surface to create highlights or corrections may cut through a paper that is too thin.

Tracing paper and drafting film provide the advantage that you avoid tracing down, or setting up your drawing on the surface, as you can work to a clearly drawn positive laid underneath. Both sides of the material can be used — for example, you can draw line work on one side and add tonal or colour detail on the reverse. This enables you to keep different elements of the rendering clean and distinct, while from the right side they appear perfectly integrated. A possible disadvantage is that, as these materials are not completely transparent, they have a cast which may show up when the artwork is photographed, so you may not be able to achieve a high white surface in a reproduction.

Artwork for reproduction

Another point to bear in mind is that reproduction requirements may limit the choice of support. Copy cameras can accept only certain sizes of artwork, and large items might need to be photographed separately. Most electronic colour scanners, which give superior results, will only accept artwork that is flexible enough to be fitted around the scanning drum.

Artwork to be reproduced on an electronic scanner that has a scanning drum must be on a support flexible enough to fit round the drum. You should also be cautious about using heavy impasto surface effects, as a thick paint layer may crack when flexed.

Illustration board surfaces are now available that can be peeled off the backing, scanned and replaced, but the range of these surfaces is limited.

Flatbed electronic scanners are a more recent innovation. The artwork is placed on a flat glass plate, which is transported over the scanning source. You should check if they are likely to be available in your area, and what size of flat artwork they will accept.

The illustration format

Traditionally, artwork has always been executed to a square or rectangular format. The eye has a circular area of vision, as does the camera lens, and circular formats might be explored, possibly vignetted or faded out at the periphery by airbrushing, to create an interesting effect. Bleeding off the edges of a rectangular illustration, which then 'floats' on the support, produces the same effect. An illustration can also be given a hard edge with a difference by breaking the rectangular frame — taking particular elements of the composition beyond the notional boundary. All these techniques help to suggest that the illustration is part of a larger reality which the observer cannot see.

MONOCHROME MEDIA AND TECHNIQUES

As in photography, it can be argued that representing form, texture and colour monochromatically is the ultimate test of your skill as an illustrator. Monochrome rendering can achieve the broadest or most detailed of effects, the technique can be interesting in its own right, and the end product is easy and cheap to reproduce.

Line and tone are the basic elements of monochrome work; you may wish to exploit one or the other in your rendering, or use a combination of the two. You may have to choose between them, particularly if it is important to represent local colour and form, or if there are limits on half-tone reproduction. Whatever the approach you adopt, the essence of a good monochrome illustration lies in the balance between light and dark: in other words, in the composition.

Line

Lines are of two types: those of constant width, which are mechanical and unsympathetic, and those of variable width, which are much more interesting and which will form a significant element of your own characteristic drawing style. Both can be drawn freehand or with a rule. The subject will probably influence the choice and style. The weight of line may also be influenced by the eventual reproduction technique, as lines and dots tend to disappear if they are not heavy enough, and they will merge if too closely spaced.

Tone

Tonal values can also be rendered in two ways: as continuous tones, using a medium that covers the support evenly, or as a pattern composed of essentially linear marks that the eye perceives as an overall tone.

Here the proposed development is drawn with ruled lines using technical pens of various widths, reflecting the precision of the facade elements (above). The existing ornate building is drawn freehand with a dip pen, a technique appropriate to its intricate weathered appearance.

Tonal variations can be achieved in line only with any kind of point medium by using hatched lines gradually increasing in density.

Point media that are relatively soft-textured, such as pencil and charcoal, can be used to create continuous tones by careful processes of shading and blending. If you use a point medium such as pencil or pen and ink to create a strong linear framework for your drawing, you can introduce tonal values in another medium sympathetic to the first. Areas of flat or graded continuous tone can be executed with ink or watercolour wash, applied with brush or airbrush, or using a dry medium such as

The surface finishes, textures and reflections are well brought out with fine hatching and dotting techniques in this precisely drawn interior. It would reproduce superbly at even a very small scale, with no need for halftone screening.

'VIKING' WALL STORAGE UNITS
DESIGNED BY ROBERT W. GILL. A.I.D.I.A.

A wax candle was lightly rubbed over the illustration board, leaving an irregular wax deposit. This was then drawn over with a fountain pen and water-soluble ink to create an interesting broken line.

powdered graphite, charcoal or pastel that can be spread and blended on the surface of the support. You can alternatively use transfer tone papers, which can be plain or graded in intensity.

The various methods of achieving tone by the visual blending of individual marks include hatching, dotting and stippling. The success of an illustration depends on your skill in handling these techniques, and in retaining the luminosity of the support surface, even in the darkest tonal areas. All of these methods are applicable to any of the point media commonly used in monochrome illustration – the various types of pencils and pens, and also charcoal, pastel, crayon or chalk.

A useful rule for hatching is that 'hatching line follows the form'. Hatching and dotting can be used to give form to a subject without necessarily using a continuous line to define its limits. The effects of

distance are generally represented by lightening the tone or reducing the weight of line, and the successful resolution of this problem in ink line, which is uniform in density, often involves using a discontinuous line or series of dots.

Individual techniques

Unconventional techniques can produce interesting results providing that you use them with discretion. For example, a very light application of wax resist to a support can be drawn over with a pen to create a textural,

This is a good example of a wax-based pencil drawing. The marks are very positive and clear, so that the illustration reproduces well. Depth is obtained by varying the strength of the pencil line and by reducing the amount of detail shown.

Delicate interior detail is beautifully brought out in this conventional graphite pencil drawing on tracing paper. The illustrator is less concerned with spatial depth than with showing details of the design.

broken line. An unusual combination of tone and texture can be produced by the technique known as frottage — when a dry medium is applied to a support laid over a textured substance which reads through the support surface. This should be used with care, as it can bring a discordant note to an otherwise unified series of techniques.

Highlights can be scratched out using a razor blade or scalpel, or may be lifted with bleach or a putty rubber, depending on the type of medium. Alternatively, they can be judiciously added using process white. Lightly scoring the surface of the support before applying a dry medium is a good way of obtaining a series of white lines in an area of otherwise continuous tone — a technique ideal for representing mortar joints, for example. You will gradually develop your own repertoire of technical tricks for particular effects.

Granular materials, such as charcoal and soft pencil, should be fixed if smudging is to be avoided. CFC-free aerosols and diffuser sprays are available. Take care to apply fixative in moderation, especially on ultra-smooth surfaces, where the medium may float off.

Graphite pencil

The conventional pencil lead is made from a mixture of graphite — a crystalline form of pure carbon, clay and plasticizers or waxes. The mixture is vitrified at high temperature: the more clay it contains, the harder the

The rough texture of the support is fully utilized in this rapid sketch in soft graphite pencil. The aim is not to show precise detail but to give a general impression of the design proposals, emphasizing the modelling of the facade.

pencil. The wax content ensures that the graphite adheres to the paper, and 'wax-based' pencils simply contain more wax than do other types. This has the disadvantage of blocking the surface fibres in the paper, so that subsequent applications to increase density slide over the top.

The range of pencil widths and grades of hardness is extensive, allowing you to produce line qualities varying from the utmost delicacy to assertive boldness. With pencil, you can render the most intricate detail or the broadest impression, with an impressive tonal range. It allows you to produce continuous tone when it is blended, it requires no drying time, and it can be easily removed. Pencil is the most versatile of all monochrome media, its main disadvantages being

that it requires fixing, and that it produces a shiny grey mark, rather than a dense black, which may not reproduce well.

As with all line media, you can suggest an idea with the minimum of effort, but there is a temptation to go for quick solutions which may result in an indecisive line or uncontrolled scribble. Conversely, you can become so seduced by the ability to depict detail that the lines become laboured and the illustration collapses through being overworked.

Be careful to avoid hard grades of pencil on very smooth surfaces, because they may not make a sufficiently dense mark, and if you exert pressure, you groove the surface, making erasure impossible. A softer grade of pencil on a rough surface may

break up the line – an effect that works with broad impressionistic effects, but is unsatisfactory in detailed subjects. Aerial perspective poses no problem, as lightness of line and tone can be achieved by varying the grade of the pencil. This is preferable to using light pressure with a soft grade pencil, which produces an indecisive mark.

Always keep the work spotlessly clean, preferably by masking areas not being worked on. Dry breadcrumbs will often remove incidental marks that you cannot work on with an eraser, which might also take out some of the drawn lines. If the pencil line is to form the basis of a watercolour illustration, the artwork should be washed in clean water to fix the line, and to remove surplus graphite that

The dense black marks obtainable with a carbon pencil are used to suggest details in this leisure pool interior, rather than to define them precisely. The marks form patterns on the support as well as conveying information.

The characteristically dense, velvety texture of charcoal provides a rich range of surface qualities, from grainy linear marks (top) to soft tonal gradations achieved by spreading the powdery medium with your fingers, a rag or a paper torchon (above).

could spread and degrade the colour.

Keep pencils sharp, otherwise you cannot make clean, decisive marks. It will save time if you prepare several pencils of the appropriate grades before you start work.

Charcoal

One of the oldest graphic media known, charcoal is produced from the partial burning of wood branches or twigs — the longer the carbonization, the softer the charcoal stick. The sticks are produced in different thicknesses and can be easily sharpened on sandpaper, but because the material is not artificially bound together, it is extremely difficult to keep work clean; if you need precise definition, it is essential to work at a large scale. Charcoal is easily blendable to produce tones, and all the usual hatching and stippling techniques can be used. You need a putty rubber for making corrections or lifting out highlights — an eraser only produces smudges which are impossible to get rid of.

The smaller sticks of compressed charcoal, with a binder added to the powdered charcoal, are slightly harder than the natural charcoal; they do not break as easily and are harder to dust off. They allow you to make broad side strokes for laying areas of tone. Charcoal pencils, which consist of compressed charcoal in a wood casing, can be used for detailed hatching and to outline forms; areas of continuous tone can be filled in with charcoal sticks.

A toothed paper gives the best results, and if you work on a tinted ground you can put in highlights with white chalk — this is an admirable combination. The charcoal mark can range from the boldest, most intense black to the most subtle, delicate grey. The medium is much undervalued and is mainly used today for preliminary design sketches, for which it is ideally suited, but remember that all charcoal work must be fixed if it is to survive in good condition.

Carbon pencil

The addition of French chalk in the graphite mixture, and the elimination of wax, provides a pencil that allows you to make a really powerful black mark, which will not blend easily. On a suitable toothed surface there is an appreciable friction between the point and the support, so that you become very conscious of the act of drawing.

The carbon pencil lead is so dense that absolutely solid blacks are obtainable, which can make for some really contrasting effects – it is altogether a tougher medium than charcoal. Again, remember to fix your work quickly, and mask off the areas that you are not working on to keep them clean.

Sanguine pencil

The sanguine Conté crayon or pencil has its devotees, but is now rarely found in architectural drawing. It is made from natural earths containing iron oxide, mixed with clay, and produces a superb, rich orange-red line which can look splendid on a tinted ground. It is much less friable than coloured pastel pencils, and well worth exploring.

White pencil

White pencil has the same composition as other types of coloured pencils (see page 57) and contains the pigment titanium oxide, which gives a bright white. For monochrome work, you can use the same techniques as for drawing with a graphite pencil, but the tonal balance is reversed – you build the image gradually from dark to light. Highly effective for night-time scenes, white pencil works best on a fairly heavily toothed dark surface, sometimes combined with white chalk, which gives stronger accents than the pencil on its own. In this type of illustration you are probably showing the effect of internal or external lighting schemes or a silhouette of the building form, rather than describing architectural details.

Dip pens

This category includes mapping pens, script pens, 'crow quill' pens, and the wide range of drawing pens with

A white wax-based pencil is used on a textured dark support in this floodlit scene. A similar result could be achieved by working in black pencil on a white support and printing the image in reverse.

Using dip pens of different nib thicknesses, as well as variations in nib pressure, produces innumerable line widths.

The patterns of brickwork, roof tiles and timber boarding are combined with shadows to define the junctions of plane surfaces (below). The boundaries are implied, rather than drawn, as we experience them in real life.

This example of free dip-pen technique (right) employs parallel hatched lines and cross-hatching. Note how the white of the support enlivens the hatched areas, although solid blacks are also used.

its place in emphasizing forms and improving composition, and it is certainly quicker to apply than dense hatching, but there is no doubt that allowing the white support to read through in very dark tonal areas enlivens the drawing. However, if your illustration is to be reproduced on a small scale, hatched lines could come together, so you can use solid black to save time.

Form can be shown not only by hatching, but by dotting and stippling, often without the need for a defining boundary line. One of the problems with a dip pen is that it is difficult to make a pattern of dots that are uniformly sized and spaced. You will be dealing with simple, often mechanical plane surfaces for the most part, where irregular stippling may be discordant.

Always consider the purposes of your drawing and preplan it in pencil. If you work on high quality illustration board, corrections can be made by scratching out quite extensively before the substrate is reached: buff any erased area with a fingernail before you draw over it, to prevent ink spread. You can clean up ends of lines with a razor blade if you find it difficult to keep hatched areas within bounds. Scratching out on paper can be almost impossible — even an electric eraser may fail to remove lines before making a hole in the paper. You may simply have to apply white correction fluid, which will remain visible on inspection and may even turn slightly yellow.

If you are drawing on film or acetate, make sure you choose an ink that bonds well with the surface. If you are using the pen line as a basis for washed-in tones or colours, it must be in waterproof ink, unless you require a deliberately blurred effect when you apply the wash

Of course, you can use fine brushes for ink line drawing, but it can be difficult to control the line thickness.

interchangeable nibs. The highly flexible nib of the traditional dip pen allows you to produce a line of variable thickness, with either waterproof or non-waterproof ink. It is this variability which compensates for the fact that all the marks you make on the paper are of uniform density, usually black. There is no possibility of gradation from black to grey, as with a pencil. It is this assured density which makes this medium so suitable for reproduction.

In outlining form or representing tone by hatching, line variation can be exploited to give life to the illustration; for not only do we read the line thickness, but at the same time we read the variation in space between

the lines. Even with ruled hatching, it is almost impossible to achieve an absolute uniformity of line thickness. You can vary the quality of line by adjusting the pressure on the nib, or by selecting from a range of different nibs, each suited to a different element of the drawing.

In order to keep an even ink flow it is essential to maintain nibs in first-class condition, keeping them free from accumulated dried ink, and not overloading them. Otherwise your ink drawing may be spoiled by unwelcome blots caused by ink flooding onto the paper, either at the ends of lines or in closely hatched work, when unwanted areas of solid black will be the result. Solid black has

This superb illustration shows the typical uniform line produced by a technical pen. It is extremely precise, yet the drawing is far from being lifeless and mechanical. Depth is indicated by the perspective lines alone, rather than by the use of diminishing line weights.

Technical pens

These pens produce lines of uniform width, quite unlike those produced by dip pens. Their tubular nibs are inflexible. You need to take a careful approach if you combine the two types of line in the same drawing, as the differing line qualities are immediately obvious. If you need to use different line widths – for differentiating foreground from background elements, for example – you can employ a battery of technical pens, each with a selected nib width. The nibs can be obtained with differing point shapes to suit formal drafting or sketching applications, and of varying hardness to suit the abrasive characteristics of the support. Whereas dip pens can be used to good effect on a rough surface, technical pens require a smooth surface. This is particularly true of fine nibs, if the ink flow to the surface is to be maintained and the delicate nib is not to 'snag', bending or breaking the tube.

These are reservoir pens, with an ink cartridge inserted in the nib unit that provides even flow. They are ideal for stippling, as the size of dot is precisely controlled and the risk of flooding is almost eliminated. Because drawings produced by technical pens have a mechanical feel to them, the use of solid blacks may not seem out of place.

The tubular nib gives a rounded end to the line, which is particularly obvious in the broader nibs. This is an indecisive mark, and you will need to square off the line end with a razor blade or scalpel – make sure the support will withstand this type of correction.

Ballpoint pens

When used on a slightly absorbent surface, a ballpoint pen can produce a uniform, very fine line. This is not very dense, however, limiting its use for reproduction, although some variation in width and density can be obtained by alterations in pressure, particularly on soft surfaces. Ball-points do not work at all if there is any grease on the surface – even grease from your skin on the paper can be sufficient to prevent ink transfer. There is virtually no friction with the surface, so that marks can be made with exceptional speed, which has to be carefully controlled if you are to produce an intelligible image.

It is almost impossible to make solid blacks, but the fine line characteristics mean that you can hatch and cross-hatch to very fine tolerances with ease. The ink flow is not perfect and you may find blots appearing occasionally. You cannot guarantee the weight of line, but its ease of use makes ballpoint a useful rendering tool for small-scale work, either in the studio or on location. Do not, however, use a ballpoint pen drawing as a basis for marker work – the marker fluid will dissolve the ink.

Fine-line markers

Combining the uniformity of line width and density of the technical pen

Ruled parallel hatching, dotting and solid blacks are evident in this simplified technical pen drawing. Ground forms and foliage are freely hatched with a dip pen. The stylized cloud forms are trued-up with a scalpel to obtain smooth curves.

Fine-line markers are very versatile. If you look closely at the line quality (below), you will see that it is more uniform than that produced by the traditional pen-and-ink technique often used for this type of subject.

and the speed of application of the ballpoint, the latest fine-line synthetic-tipped markers are among the most useful graphic tools available. The ink is either waterproof and light-resistant or water-soluble. Make sure that you are using a waterproof type if the line drawing forms a framework for application of a water-based medium. Nothing is more disheartening than to complete a detailed line drawing and then see the lines disintegrate in a grey blur when you add a wash.

The finest markers are equipped with a metal ferrule to maintain the tip thickness, and these can be used for stencilling or ruling without difficulty. They guarantee a line width of 0.08mm, and this can be reduced further by using very light pressure. Some are combined with broad nibs in the same barrel, so that a considerable variation in width is possible.

As with the technical pen, hatching and stippling can be carefully controlled because of the rigidity of the pen nib. This does not mean that

your drawing appears lifeless and mechanical, because with pressure alteration you can obtain variable impressions, but nothing like those produced by a dip pen. If you want significant line variation, you really have to use a selection of pens.

Fine-line markers can be used on

rough or smooth surfaces, but if the surface is very smooth and of low absorbency the ink may take some time to dry; on absorbent surfaces the line spreads slightly, even though the solvent evaporates very quickly. You can use bleed-proof layout paper specially prepared for marker work, but these pens are so versatile that most surfaces give good results. If you have to correct your work by scratching out, burnish the area well or the redrawn ink line will spread uncontrollably. You cannot redraw over correction mediums, so you may have to use a conventional waterproof ink and try to blend it in with the characteristic density of your marker. An alternative method of correction is to use a special blending marker to dissolve the original line, retaining the paper surface.

There is no need to think only in terms of black and white, particularly if you are not too concerned with reproduction characteristics. Among the dozens of colours available you will probably find that the browns and greys are the most suitable for architectural subjects. You can also use white markers for highlighting, or to create night-time effects, but the density and flow may not always be ideal.

Broad-line markers

These markers are excellently suited to impressions and broad-brush effects. Like fine-line markers, they are consistent and easy to use, but they have a much greater ink flow across the broad tip, so that control of the line is more difficult and line spread is almost unavoidable. You can certainly achieve some really dramatic effects because you can easily cover large areas with solid colour, either as sky tones or cast shadows and shades, but you need to plan the composition of these powerful elements in advance. You can take out the centre felts from some types of markers and use these on their sides to produce very broad strokes that cover large areas very quickly; but you will need to use masking film to obtain a clean edge. These aspects of marker work will be further described in relation to colour rendering (see page 74).

Scraperboard technique, with its sharp contrasts of black and white, can produce very powerful images. Even in this simple illustration the illustrator has used hatching and cross-hatching in a number of ways to indicate shapes and textures. It is an ideal medium for hard-edge precision work.

A dry wash of powdered graphite was used for the sky in this dramatic pencil drawing. The main elements were masked out before the graphite was rubbed into the support, and one or two cloud highlights were sharpened up by taking out the graphite with a putty eraser.

Fountain pens

The modern fountain pen has the flexibility of the dip pen in possible line variation, the smooth action of the ballpoint or fibre-tip pen, and its own cartridge-loaded ink supply. Some types can now be used with waterproof ink, and can be fitted with steel nibs for fine line work. Because they are fed from their own reservoir with an even ink flow, the risk of blotting is reduced. They are certainly very useful if you are working away from your own studio, and for impressions and small-scale work.

Scraperboard

Scraperboard, or scratchboard, has had a remarkable revival in the advertising industry, but its potential has hardly been exploited in architectural illustration. This is a pity, because the medium can be used quite freely or in a tight mechanical way; it reproduces superbly and is ideally suited to project illustration.

You can work either on a white board with a china-clay surface layer which is pre-coated with a black eggshell finish, or on a purely white board which you can block in with black ink where you need to cut away to the white areas to create tonal effects. Paint in the black areas with thin repeated coats — avoid building up a thick surface skin. Mount scraperboard on a backing board so that it does not flex and crack.

Almost all finished work is done oversize for reproduction, and it must be carefully preplanned before tracing down, as mistakes are very difficult to rectify. The beauty of the medium is that not only do you have the possibility of using ink line drawn with a pen or brush, but you are able to modify the lines by scraping them with the scraperboard tools, and to create white lines from the start as a positive element, rather than allowing them to emerge as the spaces between drawn black lines. Areas of black cross-hatching can be worked over with white cross-hatching, and vice versa, producing an infinite variation in tonal effects. With care, you can achieve results that are almost photographic, but to do so you need to work to a fairly large scale so that you can control the hatching cuts accurately — absolute precision is required for such a convincing effect. But you do not have to go to such lengths to produce effective illustrations. The technique is so direct that simplification can result in very powerful images.

The main areas of sky and buildings were put in with an airbrush to achieve the even tones required for this large rendering. Brush-painted washes could have achieved the same results, but would have been much more difficult to apply. Details were later added with pen line and small areas of ink wash.

Tonal washes

All the line media discussed here can be used for line work only, or as a basis for washes giving continuous and graded tonal values. 'Dry wash' technique can be applied using powdered graphite or granulated pastel rubbed into the surface, with softer grade material used for the darker tones, and highlights taken out with an eraser or putty rubber. You can draw charcoal lightly into the surface and blend it for the same effect. If you are working on a transparent support, such as drafting film, the tonal areas can be applied to the back and the edges cleaned up with a blade or an eraser without damage to the line work on the front.

You can apply tone as ink washes in varying strengths, bearing in mind that it is difficult to achieve an even wash with waterproof ink. Try combining waterproof and non-waterproof inks for unusual effects, using water-soluble markers, for example, which can be washed over to produce grey tones. Soft washes of watercolour in monochrome also make an excellent complement to line work, particularly sympathetic to the sensitive quality of pencil line.

A perfectly even, flat or graded tone can be applied using an airbrush — you can use any ink or paint medium that may be diluted to the right consistency. The degrees of gradation that you can achieve are infinite, but airbrushing requires masking work which can be very complex and time-consuming. The capabilities of this technique are examined in greater detail in relation to colour rendering (see pages 77-80).

Mechanical tones

There are many ranges of pre-printed mechanical tones available on self-adhesive film laminate, which you can cut out on your artwork to the shapes you wish to emphasize. Some of these are graded from light to dark. When burnished down on the surface they may not be visible from directly in front, but if they catch the light it is clear that they are not part of the original surface and this may strike a discordant note. Only use them if your work is intended for reproduction: they are best suited to the character of formal or mechanical ink line drawings done with a technical pen. Another type of pre-printed tone is the dry-transfer type that is burnished down from its backing sheet directly on the artwork, where it becomes indistinguishable from ink line work.

COLOUR MEDIA AND TECHNIQUES

Although the skilled illustrator can produce brilliant monochrome work, sometimes of great subtlety, it is undoubtedly to colour that most of us turn when we wish to present an exciting image with immediate visual impact.

When you are putting forward an illustrated proposal for appraisal, perhaps in competition with others, remember that the viewer will make a subconscious evaluation within the first few seconds, and that any further considerations will be built on this first impression. A colour rendering can make this initial message a very powerful one. With a monochrome rendering, not only does the viewer need to understand your illustration, but simultaneously to translate your image into the world of colour in which we live. This additional process dilutes the immediate impact of the rendering, so that later considerations are less dominated by the initial experience. It allows more opportunity for the material aspects of the project - how much does it cost, for example - to surface too early in the debate.

Because colour can be so powerful and seductive, competition terms often stipulate that presentations must be made in monochrome, so that judges are not swayed by technique at the expense of content.

This is not to say that colour must always be used in a particularly rich or intense way to get your message across. The vigorous application of solid tempera might be suitable for a multi-storey mega-project, but not for a small-scale housing scheme, for which a much lighter touch, with a medium such as watercolour or coloured pencil, might be more appropriate. Your choice of medium could also be influenced by the

The subject can influence the choice of medium. A large-scale commercial development (top) benefits from the bold patterns of solid colour possible with tempera, while small-scale proposals (above) are rendered in a more sympathetic coloured pencil technique.

The foreground landscape elements in this night scene are rendered in heavily textured acrylic using a brush, while the main subject is rendered more delicately with an airbrush.

surface textures you are depicting. Watercolour wash or airbrushing for glazed areas might be combined with tempera for rough brickwork and heavily applied acrylic for foreground landscaping.

You should also consider the permanence of your illustration. Many pigments may be only moderately lightfast. Watercolours eventually fade if exposed to natural light, and marker drawings change colour and can almost disappear in a matter of weeks. If your illustration is for immediate use only, this will be of no consequence; but your client may want to hang it on the boardroom wall. So make sure that you know the end-use of your work.

Making corrections

You should also think about the problems of correcting your work. You may be involved in illustrating a project where design changes are still being made; you may be trying out a new technique which you have not fully mastered; your household pet may walk across your graded wash while you are cleaning your brushes.

You can correct some media by sponging out with water or spirit, with plenty of blotting paper on hand, and the support must be substantial enough to withstand this treatment.

With watercolours and markers which stain the surface, often the only way is to cut out a section of the support and patch in a new area. Try to do this along definite lines in the picture so that the joins can be lost. In correcting gouache work, in particular, large areas must be completely overpainted if you are to avoid a 'tide mark' effect where your new work stops.

If you have problems with pick-up from the paint surface below, and it is not possible to sponge it out neatly, a spray of matt fixative over the area to be redone will seal the surface and allow you to paint over it. Mask out finished areas so that they will not be affected. Working over tempera should pose no problems provided that later mixes are kept fairly dry, and acrylics, which dry rapidly and can be overpainted immediately, pose no problems at all.

Masking techniques

Unless you are using a sketch technique, where an impression rather than a hard-edged representation is called for, you will need to be precise in the application of your medium. Masking out areas which you do not wish to work on is a great help and can be done in two ways.

Masking fluid is a natural rubber latex in a solvent, usually coloured with a yellow dye so that you can see where it is being applied. If this is put on with a brush or pen over areas to be masked out, you can readily apply your washes of colour evenly to the support without the necessity to concentrate on achieving a sharp edge. The masking material is then peeled off by rubbing with a finger or soft eraser. Before you apply masking fluid to an important piece of artwork, check that it will peel off easily from the support you intend to use - it can be difficult to remove from some porous surfaces. As a general rule, do not leave it on the support any longer than is absolutely necessary.

This material is not only useful for

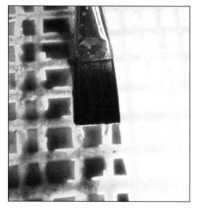

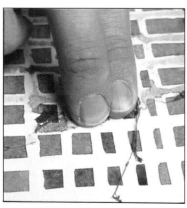

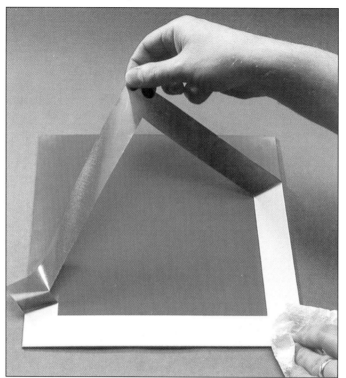

Masking film is ideal for giving a crisp edge to geometric shapes and areas of graded tone. It provides complete cover with the advantage that its transparency allows you to match colours and tones against areas you have previously painted as the work progresses.

Masking fluid provides a form of hard-edged masking easily applied to irregular shapes and fine details that would be difficult to cut out of masking film. The fluid is painted on (top) and allowed to dry to a rubbery surface film; you can then wash over it freely with a water-based paint (above centre); and simply rub away the masking once the colour has dried (above).

defining the edges of large areas, it is ideal for showing tree structures, lamp standards, railings and other fine work against darker backgrounds without having to use body colour. Be careful if you are using masking fluid with gouache. In rubbing away the latex you will almost certainly burnish the adjacent paint surface, and this cannot be corrected.

Masking film is the more practical material for architectural work. This transparent low-tack material is laid down over the artwork and lightly rubbed down, and the areas to be masked are cut out with a sharp scalpel, taking care not to cut into the surface below. The paint is applied, allowed to dry slightly, and the film removed. On textured supports the film may not adhere tightly to the surface and watercolour, in particular, may run under the edge; in this case it is better to use masking fluid. If you have to apply the film over previously painted gouache do not press it down too hard, as it may pull the paint surface away when it is removed. As with masking fluid, check a small area to see if the film can be removed without pulling up the surface.

You do not always have to mask out to achieve a clean edge. If your support is heavy enough you can use the back of a scalpel or a knife to score the outline of areas of different colour. Any wash you apply will stop at the indentation. The disadvantage is that the groove may hold additional pigment, resulting in a dark perimeter line. This is particularly true of sedimentary washes.

In coloured pencil and pastel work a simple way to obtain a tidy edge at speed is to place a straight-edge on the boundary line and run your strokes up to it. You can then concentrate on applying the colour, without having to worry about terminating the marks neatly.

Drying and fixing

You will often be working to tight deadlines, so drying times are important. A good way to speed up the drying process is to use a hairdryer, preferably one with a cool setting. Do not overheat your paint surface as the support may warp, and the bond between the paint and its support, and even the permanency of the paint itself, may be affected. Above all, do

Loose, broad pencil strokes for the foreground complement the free coloured ink details in this delightful Japanese illustration.

This fine drawing of proposals for Genoa shows the detail possible with tightly controlled pencil techniques.

not heat up masking film. The adhesive will become more tacky, making it almost impossible to remove without damaging the paint.

You must fix pastel work to make it permanent, but you can also use spray fixatives to protect artwork. This can be matt, semi-gloss or high gloss. Your illustration may receive rough treatment – it is surprising how quickly the edges become covered in finger marks. Note that spray fixatives can darken tones if applied too heavily. This is particularly true of gouache, on which you can use this technique deliberately to great effect to intensify tonal contrasts.

Coloured pencil

Coloured pencils are made from clay, or similar 'extender', pigments, binders, hardeners and wax. The hardener is used because these pencils cannot be kiln-fired, as graphite pencils are. Many traditional inorganic pigments are no longer in use because of their chemical composition, and great efforts are made to ensure that the pigments now used, both traditional and synthetic, are ground as finely as possible to

avoid scratching and are exceptionally lightfast. As with paint pigments, the higher the quality, the higher the cost of production. The wax makes the pigment stick to the support, and if there is too much the surface indentations fill up more easily, making subsequent applications of colour more difficult. Coloured pencils do not erase as easily as graphite pencils, and carefully

scraping back to the support surface may be the only way of removing dense colour. If you have to use an eraser make sure that you keep it clean. It soon picks up pigment which can be transferred to unwanted areas.

Because this is a point medium, work can take a long time; but this very slowness means that you can control the progress of the work very precisely, not only in the way you

Few colours are used in this example of a complex interior, but the variation in pencil strokes and their juxtaposition builds up a colour blend which at a distance appears as a uniform colour.

apply the colour but also where you apply it. The medium is so versatile that you can make a tight drawing or a very loose one. Differing point shapes, pressures and ways of holding the pencil all affect line quality. A chisel point gives an instant change from narrow to broad strokes; 'fat lead' pencils, with leads up to 4mm wide, give extra-wide strokes suitable for large areas, where the use of thin hard leads could be very laborious; square uncased pigment sticks can be used for large areas of 'underpainting', and a mark made with the stick on edge can give a sharp line.

Supports should have moderate 'tooth'. If they are too rough pigment will be deposited on the top of the textured surface, leaving white in the hollows. This makes it difficult to obtain saturated colours. Choose a happy medium, where all the pigment is transferred, but just enough support is visible to give sparkle to your drawing. Coloured supports, which can unify a composition by the imposition of an overall colour regime, will markedly affect the colour of the translucent pigment. As with

watercolour the characteristics of the support should be used in a positive way. Tracing paper or drafting film, if not too smooth, make ideal supports. You can work on both sides, or on the reverse only, to achieve really subtle differences in colour and tone. You can easily scratch out on them, but be careful not to cut through the matt surface on film if you need to draw over the area again - the pigment will not adhere to the shiny substrate.

The greatest problem is in obtaining tonal contrast, because of the translucency of the pigment and the virtual impossibility of obliterating the support. This characteristic gives illustrations great delicacy. Always work from light to dark; it is easy to modify light colours to darken them, but very difficult to modify dark ones.

You can apply the colour in different ways. Highly saturated colour requires high pressure on the pencil, and low saturation needs low pressure. The simplest application is to use single colours in varying densities, taking a pencil straight from the box for each colour you need. If this is the only method you use, you

will need a vast selection of colours to cover all your requirements. Because of the translucency of the pigment it is possible to use layering - applying one colour over another - to obtain flat areas of colour which are much more vibrant. A more subtle technique is to cross-hatch one colour over another, allowing the support to show through - yellow hatched over blue produces an apparent green while retaining the distinctness of the constituent colours on close inspection.

All the techniques of hatching, cross-hatching and dotting used in monochrome are also applicable to coloured pencil work. For large areas of just one colour, hatching provides a much more interesting surface than simply laying the colour solidly over the support. At a distance it may not be seen as hatching at all. Applying short strokes or dots of different colours side by side again produces this effect of 'optical mixing'. By using hatching or dotting in this way you are indicating texture, colour and form at the same time. The techniques are laborious, but the results are well worth it. A further technique is to

In this Hong Kong landscape, the illustrator uses different colour saturations to emphasize distance and to pick out important elements.

A scalpel has been used extensively here (left) to scrape out window and sunscreen frames.

apply colours side by side and blend them with solvent, using a torchon. Whatever you do, avoid the muddy effect often produced by applying colours over each other in dense, solid layers.

Heavy, superimposed colour layers can be scraped back or scratched to reveal the colour layer or the support underneath. This technique is known

as 'sgraffito', and is best applied on a board support. Textured effects can be achieved, and if the colour is scraped with the flat side of a blade, the pigment forms smooth areas of flat colour with a slight sheen, useful for showing highly polished surfaces. Mortar joints and window glazing bars can easily be scraped out to show as light lines set against a darker

Pastels are applied freely over a line drawing to produce colour blends of great subtlety. The roughness of the surface allows the white support to show through. This, combined with the superimposed layering of the pastels, produces a strikingly luminous effect, in a very personal style.

background. Fine lines can also be made by impressing grooves into the support with a hard point, working through tracing paper rather than on the support itself. Lightly applied colour does not get into the grooves, which remain visible as the colour of the support.

Blending colours by rubbing hard with a torchon or white pencil again produces a smooth, shiny surface, which can represent steel or glass surfaces, or highlights on circular forms. The pressure of the burnishing completely breaks up the granulations in the pigment, forcing it into the support. Note that burnishing with a white pencil also modifies the colour.

Water-soluble pigments can be laid down and dissolved with water or blended with turpentine or marker blenders. They are hard to erase because the pigment soaks into the support, and it is difficult to predict the results. They heighten the intensity of the colour by eliminating the white support which shows through dry pigmentation, and they can be worked over when dry with normal pencils. They do not give very satisfactory results when used entirely on their own for finished work.

Be careful when fixing your illustration. If you apply fixative too liberally the wax in the pigment mix will dissolve, producing unwanted colour blending. If you find that a wax haze appears on your drawing, wipe it off carefully with a dry cloth and then fix it - it should not recur.

A carefully controlled use of masking is the basis of this dry-wash pastel illustration. The support has very little texture, so the masked areas can be sharply defined, and the 'washes' are very flat. The stylized figures are the hallmark of this accomplished illustrator.

Pastel

This is a surprisingly underused medium for architectural illustration. The pigments, which are the same as those used for oil and watercolour paints, are mixed with chalks, clays and a binder to form round- or square-section sticks. The more binder in the composition and the greater the pressure used to form the sticks, the harder they are. The intensity of the colour depends on the amount of chalk used and more binder means less brilliant colour. Black pigment is added for the darker colours. There is no wax to make the pigment adhere to the support, and the powdery surface must be fixed for durability.

The traditional pastel sticks are undoubtedly messy to use, and can fracture unexpectedly. Pastel pencils, with more binder to strengthen the lead, are cleaner but do not give the broad strokes possible with the sticks.

It is often thought that pastel work must be at a large scale. This is not necessarily true, for while broad effects of sky and landscape can be easily put in with pastel sticks, building detail can be rendered with the pencils, producing a hard-edge illustration with intense colours.

There are dozens of colours available, each with several tints. You should take advantage of the potential for overlaying and hatching to produce effects of tremendous subtlety by working with as broad a selection as possible. The range varies from the lightest of tints to brilliant primaries and rich dark colours, but they all have the particular quality which comes from the flakes of pigment reflecting the light. You can build up colour very thickly (impasto) for dramatic contrasts, as there is no wax to prevent a layer adhering to the one beneath.

If you need to correct your work you can scrape off unwanted pigment with the side of a blade, finish with an eraser, and spray lightly with fixative if you have damaged the surface. Never try to remove pastel with a hard eraser: always use a kneadable eraser formed to a point to lift off the pigment. Brush any loose pigment away with a soft paintbrush, a compressed-air canister or a vacuum attachment – wiping it off will smudge the pastel.

Like coloured pencils, pastels require a toothed surface for pigment transfer, and there are papers made especially for pastel work. You must strike a balance between using a support which will retain plenty of pigment and one smooth enough to allow you to define your subject precisely at a small scale. The very fine sandpapers available for pastel work are really too coarse for architectural rendering.

Even more than in coloured pencil work, coloured supports are of great value in unifying an illustration, whether they are light or dark in tone, or warm or cool in colour. You can use the coloured support to show through in hatched work, or in its own right, to define some of the major elements in the composition.

While hatching, cross-hatching and dotting are the stock-in-trade of the pastel illustrator, the effects will be quite different from those obtained with coloured pencils, as the pastel line is broader and less continuous. The principle of allowing one colour to be read through another remains. You can layer colours one over the other, either by making individual strokes or by using solid colour, but if you use too much pressure you may drag the lower pigment across the surface, mixing it with the top colour and degrading both. A great advantage of the pastel stick is that you can use it on its side to make very broad strokes and cover large areas rapidly, but this should not be overdone: too great an area of one colour of the same texture can be very uninteresting.

An alternative technique is to use powdered pastel as a dry wash, rubbed into the support. You lose the characteristic fragility of the surface, but gain enormously in your freedom to produce areas of flat or graded colour, rather like a 'dry airbrush' finish. Use a torchon, or paper blender, if you wish to work in small areas of colour. Highlights can be taken out precisely with a hard eraser, and textures can be added either by superimposing individual pastel marks or pressing larger pastel grains into the surface of wet fixative. Fine detail can be added over the fixed pastel with graphite or coloured pencils. The success of this technique depends entirely on careful masking, using masking film or detail paper. Each pastel layer must be fixed with

Very precise masking and dry wash applied to the building are combined with a loose pastel technique in the foreground to give an almost photorealist quality. The free and disciplined uses of the medium are effectively complementary.

matt fixative before you apply later masks, and the sequence of operations must be carefully planned.

Whether you are using this technique or the more traditional methods, be careful when you are spraying your fixative. Fixative can be applied in stages to protect work in progress, and when the illustration is complete. Do not apply it too heavily or pigment may be displaced and colours darkened. If you are using a thin support, try spraying it from the back; the fixative will soak through without affecting the surface brilliance of the pigment.

Oil pastel

Oil pastels are made with an oil binder, and are an altogether heavier medium. They make thick strokes of rich colour, and come in a limited colour range. They are not suitable for detailed work, being seen at their best in large-scale sketches, and they do not overlay well if you are interested in colour mixing. They will dissolve in white spirit or turpentine for colour blending, but you need to select a substantial support if you adopt this technique. In short, a medium more for experimentation and perhaps mixed media use.

Conté crayons

These small square-section sticks are similar to pastels, but a slightly different composition and drying method makes them harder. They are oily, but not sticky like oil pastels, and will take on very smooth surfaces. They were originally made in black, white and one or two earth colours, but are now available in a wide colour range. They can give broad side strokes or fine lines, and are suitable for all the hatching and colour blending techniques of pastels. Because of the oil binder they are not as brilliant as pastels, but they are cleaner to use, and could provide an interesting alternative.

Gouache

This is simply opaque water-based paint, made from pigment and a binder – gum arabic, starch or a synthetic substance. Nearly all colours contain white for opacity, but some manufacturers use a very dense concentration of pigment without the white. This is fine for the darker colours, but you really need to add white to bring out the brilliance of the pigment in the lighter ones. Gouache has a special attraction for illustrators, for the dense flat colours reproduce well; they are often referred to as 'designers' colours'. The pigments used in making gouache are graded for lightfastness. Some colours, such as burnt umber, burnt sienna, cerulean blue and viridian, are extremely permanent. Others, like magenta and the violets, are fugitive. There are a few colours which are not opaque – some oranges, yellows and viridian are either partly or wholly transparent.

Because of the opacity of gouache in general, it is a valuable medium for photomontage and retouching work, applied either with a brush or an airbrush. There are some colour ranges in which the pigment is ground

The buildings are carefully defined, and coloured in a dry-wash technique. The landscape elements are put in with oil pastels and the combination of scratching out and impressing loose pigment into the surface gives an interesting texture which contrasts with the smooth surfaces of the buildings.

This rendering in gouache is typical of the medium. Areas of solid flat colour are built up with subsequent detail to form a powerful composition.

The precise detail and covering power possible with gouache make it ideal for photomontage work (below). All the main surfaces were masked so that the paint could be applied with high definition to match the photographic qualities.

even more finely than usual, especially for airbrushing. Unless you are very meticulous and regularly clean the caps of your paint tubes, you will find that the paint has a fairly short shelf life. Paint in the neck of the tube soon solidifies if the cap does not fit tightly. You may also find that your brushes have a short life too, particularly the fine ones, as gouache can be a heavy medium to work with. You may find it more economical to use synthetic brushes and to throw them away after one or two projects, than to try to get good value from expensive brushes which soon lose their points.

The gouache colour range includes metallics, fluorescents, and the yellow, cyan and magenta process colours, They dry quickly with a matt, chalky finish, which takes on a patina when rubbed. It is best to protect work in progress to avoid this. Because gouache is water-soluble, overpainting can dissolve the paint layer underneath, mixing the pigments, a phenomenon known as 'pick-up'. This is particularly the case

if you overpaint with a mix which is too wet. This is the major drawback to an excellent medium, but by the addition of an acrylizing medium - a polymer resin - to your first paint layer the problem can be overcome, as it makes the paint water-resistant. Wash out your brush and palette

immediately or the paint on them will dry hard. You can also paint onto uncoated acetate with this method.

Too heavy an application of paint can lead to cracking and the paint may come away from the surface. This is made worse with a support which is too flexible, so many illustrators use a

board support. A little gum arabic in the paint mix will help. Certain pigments have a tendency to 'migrate'. Some of the strong synthetic colours will bleed through into any superimposed paint, and also stain the support. A typical example would occur in white glazing bars painted over glass areas containing blue pigment. If you have to correct work of this nature try using bleed-proof white. This will stop further colour migration and you can then paint over it, or you can use it on its own. A carefully controlled spray of fixative can have the same effect. Corrections can easily be made by dampening with a sponge and lifting off the colour with a moist brush or blotting paper. Heavy pigment should first be scraped away with the side of a blade.

Virtually any support is usable, provided it is not greasy. Because gouache does not flow as easily as watercolour you will find that using a very rough support, while giving textural opportunities, will be quite hard work. Gouache is so opaque that it covers coloured supports well, and you can use this background colour to play a major part in the composition, just as with pastel. If you apply the colour in thin washes remember that

the colour of the support will modify the apparent colour of the diluted pigment. For high-definition work a smooth line board is ideal, but this does not take diluted washes easily unless you dampen the surface first. This can lead to differential drying and board distortion. In any case, paint on a non-absorbent surface takes longer to dry - do not be tempted to overdo it with the hairdryer!

You can combine wet-in-wet techniques - for skies and distant landscape, for example - with a bolder approach for your main building subject. If you use only a little water the brilliance of the pigment is brought out, while dilution produces soft, translucent effects. Colours change if diluted, not because of change in the pigment but because the support surface is visible in varying degrees. In all cases the paint colour lightens as it dries. Note the effect of the support colour - the same pigment appears lighter on a dark ground than it does on a light one.

With care you can work from dark to light almost as easily as from light to dark. If you underpaint with dilute washes, which sink into the support and will not be disturbed by later applications of paint, pick-up should

Opaque gouache covers coloured supports well, a property exploited in this night-time scene (above).

Grass and road textures were obtained in this case (below) by using an almost dry bristle brush, rather than by random spattering.

not occur. For a heavy uniform wash with no brush marks, mix colour to a thin creamy consistency and apply the wash to an absolutely level support. This will give you an area of flat colour typical of the medium. If you need to reduce the intensity of a colour, always start with white and add the colour to form the tint, never add white to the colour, to avoid wasting pigment. To obtain darker shades, add black to the colour, gradually lowering the value. Zinc white will give you the clearest and most lightfast tints; permanent white will give you the greatest opacity. Different blacks will give intense black, grey or brown top tones, and make cool or warm greys.

There are many ways of achieving texture over pre-painted flat colour. For dry-brush technique, load a brush with pigment and work it out on spare paper until hardly any colour remains, then draw the almost dry brush over the surface to create an intermittent pigment deposition. This is ideal for hinting at tree foliage in front of your building, without picking up the paint or smearing it. With a rough surface this technique can produce sparkling highlights on water or broken cloud effects. Drawing a knife blade across loaded toothbrush bristles produces a random spattering, useful for brickwork, grass and road surfaces. A stiff bristle brush loaded with almost dry colour and applied vertically can give you a highly controlled stipple. Spraying with an atomizer gives you an even finer, uniform texture. You can even mix texture paste with the paint to give extra weight for a foreground impasto treatment.

You will need to use masking if you are spattering or spraying. You will also find it of help when painting areas of graded colour, which are particularly difficult to apply if you are working with really dense pigment. Because the gouache dries quickly you may not have time to bring your work

In this mixed-media rendering (above) hand-painted gouache is used to superimpose elements at ground level over an airbrushed base. The opaque medium allows you to put in very fine detail without difficulty, which here contrasts well with the lighter treatment of the building behind.

An almost dry brush loaded with white was drawn lightly across the surface to produce highlights on the water.

to a clean edge and still apply the paint fast enough to avoid drying marks. This could lead to reworking and an unsightly build-up of pigment. Masking out means that you can concentrate on the painting, even mixing colour on the support if necessary, letting the edges take care of themselves.

Gouache is very suitable for mixed media work, with ink or watercolour, when its solid colour characteristics can be used in contrast to advantage.

Tempera

This medium uses the same body colour pigments as gouache, but incorporates egg or similar protein, such as casein, as a binder, with additional drying oil. These form an emulsion which can be diluted with water. Tempera gives results very similar to gouache, and is sometimes mistaken for it, but it dries very quickly, and when hard it is almost permanent, being virtually insoluble. Some artists prefer to mix their own egg-tempera colours, but several manufacturers now produce tempera colour in tubes and jars, not necessarily with an egg base. Products are sometimes labelled as being tempera, or have tempera and gouache on the same label, when they appear to be gouache colours, so make sure that the ones you buy are oil emulsions with the essential drying properties of tempera.

The paint becomes lighter when dry, as does gouache, and it will not crack or discolour. Its great advantage over gouache is that it can be overpainted when dry without risk of pick-up. Its great disadvantage is that it can dry even faster, so that it is difficult to work the colours on the support – to achieve graded colour, for example. You may have to use cross-hatching with a fine brush to make gradual colour changes, or place narrow bands of slightly differing colours side by side, to build up a colour change in facets.

You can use the same supports as you would use for gouache, but you will need a non-absorbent palette, and you should wash your brushes frequently, or suspend them in water, if they are not to dry hard. Once the paint layer is dry you will have to make corrections by overpainting, as the paint film can only be removed with difficulty. It is not easy to damage the dried surface, and it will take a slight polish if buffed with a soft cloth. The

The drying characteristics of tempera allow for rapid overpainting without the previous paint layers being disturbed. Although this rendering must have taken many hours, it gives the impression of having been dashed off rapidly. Any attempt to 'clean up' the painting would have completely destroyed its spontaneous feel.

rapid drying and possibilities for overpainting mean that you have great scope for spontaneous illustration, quickly applying one colour over another. The colour dries with more sparkle than gouache. This can give a tempera illustration a more lively feel than that given by the generally more sedate gouache approach.

Acrylic

This is the most technically advanced painting medium available. Traditional pigments are used, together with many new synthetics, held in a tough, flexible acrylic polymer base. Prussian blue, alizarin crimson and viridian are not used as the pigments are not compatible with the acrylic. Some types of acrylic paint are soft and easily brushed out, others are rather like oil colour, but all are diluted with water. They dry very quickly and can be painted over without pick-up. Their main disadvantage is that they have a residual tack which collects dirt, so that finished work should be protected.

Manufacturers' ranges vary from thirty to over eighty colours, including iridescent ones. To combat rapid drying, which occurs through chemical change as well as water evaporation, retarders can be added. The more dilute the paint, the less effective are the retarders. Some formulations have a quick drying time when brushed out but have an extended palette life, but you will still find that your colour dries out too quickly if you do not use a disposable paper palette liner system, which can

The illustrator handles acrylics in two different ways here. The background is put in with thin washes reminiscent of watercolour, and for the main subject a more robust technique with a heavier paint mix is used.

The application of thin acrylic washes allows the support to show through and emphasizes the translucency of the medium. This illustrator uses a highly textured support, but still achieves precision in the important areas.

be kept damp. It is best to use synthetic brushes, as they will withstand vigorous cleaning, and you can keep them suspended in water so that they do not dry out.

Almost all supports are suitable, including coloured ones. Alterations are simple – paint out the offending area in white and start again. The medium is essentially opaque, but can be diluted to give very thin washes. These can look very like watercolour, but blending and colour gradation can be difficult to achieve because of the quick drying time. Dilute washes can be superimposed and still retain the clarity and purity of the colour underneath, a characteristic very useful for superrealist illustration. There is little change in tone as the paint dries, so you can easily predict your final colour effects. You can work wet-in-wet using the paint straight from the tube, but for large areas such as skies it is advisable to add a gel retarder to stop the paint drying too quickly. It is easy to work from dark to light, so you do not have to plan your painting as carefully as you would a watercolour. To achieve solid colour, use a series of washes to build up a flat opaque surface, rather than apply paint heavily in one layer. This will

maintain the translucency that is such a feature of the medium.

You can mix gloss or matt acrylic mediums with the paint. These increase translucency and promote even flow and distribution of the pigment in a diluted wash, which will produce a thin, smooth paint layer. Simply thinning with water may not ensure this. Addition of matt medium also gives a matt surface finish. With either of these mediums, used either on their own or with minimum pigment, you can build up transparent glazes that give great depth and

brilliance to the paint beneath. Gel medium is much thicker and can be used to carry extra colour for impasto work, and to increase colour translucency. There are also water tension breakers, or wetting agents, which are particularly useful additions to your mixing water when you need to apply watercolour-type washes. Large areas of flat or graded wash are much easier to apply than in watercolour, as the acrylic medium is more bulky and manageable than a pure water wash.

Because the dry paint is impervious

In this Lisbon interior (below) the use of drybrush painting over thin acrylic washes brings out the texture of the support and adds sparkle to the illustration.

This bold application of opaque acrylic paint over a coloured support shows how exciting the medium can be when used with confidence.
The stylized representation of the trees, using free brush strokes, contrasts effectively with the careful representation of the building.

it is ideal for repeated masking out with film, as the surface will not pull away with the film when you remove it. Hard-edge illustration is therefore no problem. With no pick-up to worry about, and a fast drying time, you can overpaint detail such as brick jointing in minutes. With tight deadlines, acrylic really comes into its own. All the hatching, dotting, stippling and spattering techniques described for gouache and tempera can be used. Texture paste, even sand, can be added to the paint to give heavy foreground texture. You can use dry brush strokes to create sparkle; an even dryer brush scrubbed into the surface will thin out the pigment and create delicate mist-like effects, useful for subduing background detail and adding atmosphere. The medium is so tough that you can attack the support with as much vigour as you would wish. Once you have mastered the art of mixing the various additives with the paint, you will find acrylic is extremely versatile; it can provide a colour range from the most vibrant to the most subtle, with exceptional clarity; you can produce finished work with great speed. In short, this is an ideal medium for the hard-pressed illustrator.

Watercolour

This has long been a favourite medium of the architectural renderer. The feeling of spontaneity, clarity of colour and translucency make it a perfect medium for illustrating sunlit objects in the landscape. The pigment is bound with gum arabic for adhesion and glycerine for improved flow. It is available in cakes or tubes, and concentrated, though more fugitive, liquid colours can be obtained in jars, some with their own droppers to transfer the colour to your palette for further mixing. Some colours, such as alizarin crimson, stain the support and always leave a mark. Others, such as cerulean blue, are actually opaque.

The transparent quality of the majority of pigments means that you should work from light to dark, and to realize the medium's full potential you should always make sure that the support can be read through the paint layers. Careful pre-planning is essential to preserve the white areas you will need. Any attempt to put in areas of light tone using body colour will only end in disaster, except for the most delicate final highlights, which can be applied with opaque white.

If you draft out your illustration in pencil, remember that as soon as you paint over the line you will not be able to erase it, and it will be visible through the transparent pigment. If

Watercolour is the ideal medium for capturing the diffused light typical of temperate climates (above).

Maintaining the white of the support requires careful planning if you are to use the translucency of the medium to best advantage.

this worries you, try tracing down with photo-blue tracing-down paper. This will not be as visible, and will be lost in reproduction. The alternative is to project your draft onto the support with an overhead projection.

The medium's main disadvantage in commercial work is that because of the transparency and low deposition of the pigment in diluted washes, it may not reproduce well. All your delicate colour variations may be lost under the camera. The second disadvantage is that although nothing could be quicker than applying a colour wash, you must wait until the first wash is hard dry before applying another one. For a rapid sketch this poses no problem, but if you are

building up your finished work with a number of superimposed washes, it can take a long time. It pays to have two or three illustrations under way at the same time, so that you can move from one to the other as they are drying. Never use a dryer unless the paint is in the final stages of drying naturally.

The whole basis of watercolour technique is the application of colour washes, but do not overdo this. Too many washes will totally obscure the support, you will lose the depth and transparency and end up with a degraded opaque colour. You would have been better advised to use a body colour medium to start with.

There are three main types of

You must develop a flawless technique if you are to use washes successfully. There should be no uneven pigment settlement or 'tide marks'. You can see examples of graded and sedimentary washes in this illustration, in which body colour has also been used for incidental foreground detail.

Wet-in-wet technique can be seen in the sky in this rendering of an urban site. It is difficult to predict the exact result of this method, but in sky and landscape areas precise definition of surface qualities may not be important.

work they may distort. If the paper is heavy enough it can be taped down, but it is safer to stretch all watercolour supports. However much water you use, stretched paper will always return to an absolutely flat surface. Most supports are white, but you can also use lightly tinted papers. They will affect the brilliance of your colours, but help in establishing tonal relationships.

You can apply the paint in various ways. Working wet-on-dry means that you have absolute control of the medium and can paint with crisp outlines. You can work wet-on-damp, where the colour will spread more easily, resulting in slightly diffused edges. Working wet-in-wet, colour diffuses into the wet support or into the previous wet wash in a quite unpredictable manner. You can use this as a starting point for more conventional superimposed washes and for the addition of detail. The essentially fluid quality of effortless application must be maintained for success, so use as large and as fully charged a brush as possible, and develop a free movement of your arm and wrist, rather than relying on the flexibility of your fingers. Be patient in allowing your paint to dry. If you try to work over a damp surface layer you will end up with blotches and muddy colours.

support suitable for watercolour. A line board with a highly finished, ironed surface incorporating china clay is fine for very detailed hard-edge work, but the colour stays on the surface and can be difficult to manage. You can counter this to some degree by adding gum arabic to the palette. This gives the paint more body

without affecting the colour. Hot-pressed papers are moderately smooth, and 'not', or cold-pressed, papers are quite rough. The roughness affects the overall colour because of the amount of white left in the paper's indentations. Many papers can be pre-bonded to boards, but if you are involved in a great deal of heavy wash

The treatment of sky and building facades in this Osaka Trade Centre presentation show the watercolour graded wash at its best. The illustrator's technique is as impressive as the architecture!

The basis of successful watercolour work is the wash. Work with the support slightly tilted, not level as with gouache, and always mix more colour than you will need. Apply the paint with fully charged, even, horizontal strokes. You can use a damp sponge rather than a brush, but slightly dampen your support first. Grade the wash if necessary by adding water, working from dark to light, and keep stirring the paint in the palette so that the pigment does not settle. If the support is very rough you will obtain a 'broken wash' by gently laying the wash over the top surface. Interesting texture results from adding heavier pigments which settle out rapidly to form granulated washes. You can build up tone and change colours with repeated washes. Keep some blotting paper handy, just in case the colour runs in unexpected directions, but never interfere with a wash once you have started it. You may be able to amend it when it is quite dry, but often

In this delicate rendering the fine detail of material joints and edges of surfaces are drawn in pencil, yet they do not dominate the composition.

it is much better to start again if something has gone wrong.

All sorts of special effects are possible. You can produce rough texture with drybrush technique. Spattering, dotting and stippling can be used, and if these are done on a damp surface the marks run together to give interesting soft marbling effects, useful for detailing surface

finishes. A much more random effect is obtained by mixing the wash with solvents, which repel the water and produce variable pigment settlement. Working over a wax resist, such as candle wax, produces broken colour, useful for tree trunks, foliage and dappled ground shadows. Cloud forms can be sponged out, wet or dry; highlights can be scraped out with a

The illustrator decided to use a strong ink line (left) to define forms before applying the watercolour washes. In this case the drawing is as important as the painting.

This diagrammatic panorama (below) uses a fine line to define areas which are then filled in with flat watercolour washes. This creates an illustration which is as informative as it is refined.

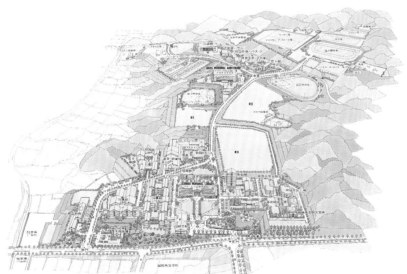

watercolour using a ruling pen or a fine brush. These should never dominate the surface. Heavy ink line, in particular, can kill the lightness of an otherwise successful composition. The deliberate planning of your rendering as a line-and-wash drawing is another matter. You can draw the line work first in pencil or waterproof ink, and fill in the areas in wash, or you can lay the wash drawing first and then outline it. Because you are using a point medium, your support must be reasonably smooth if you are to obtain good line quality.

You can use the line not only as a boundary line for your colour, but by using differing line thicknesses and hatching you can indicate tone, form and texture, so that the line drawing can almost stand on its own. If you draw over a wet area the ink line bleeds slightly, and this helps in aerial perspective. Because so much of the drawing structure is carried by the line, you can concentrate on filling in areas with flat, dilute colour washes to indicate surface colour and shadows. Any tricks of sedimentation or texturing are superfluous. The interest is in the interplay between the fine line and the purity of the watercolour.

blade or scrubbed out with a bristle brush, or even sandpaper. In working from light to dark, use masking fluid applied with a fine brush or, better, with a pen, for delicate shapes which can be freely painted over. The light areas can be used for the application of luminous spot colour - flowers in the landscape area, for example.

If you are using a smooth or only slightly toothed support, on which masking film can be applied with a firm edge, you can lift off colour with a

sponge in precisely defined areas, for reflections in polished surfaces, highlights on circular columns, or for cones of artificial light. The edges can be carefully softened with a damp brush when the film is removed. You can also use a sponge and blotting paper to correct work, but make sure that you protect work in progress.

Because the finished paint surface is so flat, construction joints and other fine detail can be drawn in on completion with pencil or ink, or in

Markers

Marker pens, with their self-contained coloured ink supply, are ideal for rapid project visualization, and can be used quite satisfactorily for certain types of finished work. Most of them have a solvent-based ink reservoir, are waterproof, and are produced in vast graded colour selections, some with an exceptionally wide range of warm and cool greys. Markers can have broad, medium, fine or ultra-fine points, sometimes combined in the same pen. The ultra-fine pens, with the point encased in a metal ferrule, are suitable for precision line work. A limited range of very wide markers is produced, but is difficult to obtain – if you need very broad strokes you can remove the ink-soaked felt from inside the screw-top type and use it on its side. This particular range also features sets of architects' outdoor, wood and stone colours.

You can also obtain water-based markers, generally with fine points, and sometimes with brush tips. You can use both types on the same drawing. Marker ink is generally transparent, so you must work from light to dark, but there are acrylic-based fluorescent, metallic and white markers which are opaque. They are not lightfast, so you should use them only for rapid impressions or for illustrations to be reproduced, when permanence is not required. When marker ink is fully dry, pick-up is unlikely to happen, although this can vary with the brand.

Supports with different absorption rates give different colour strengths, and those which are too open-textured allow ink to bleed into the fibres, so that it is hard to maintain crisp edges. The ink soaks right through thinner papers, but special bleed-proof marker paper is coated on the reverse to prevent this. One advantage of thin supports is that you can apply the colour directly over an

Markers are ideal for impressionistic illustrations. Fine and broad markers are used here with exciting abandon, stimulating the viewer's interest in the project without indicating specific design details.

This market hall scene is rendered on a smooth-surfaced illustration board to minimize marker spread. Fine-point water-based and broad spirit-based markers were used, outlined with a fine black marker. Distant colours were subdued by scraping them out with the flat edge of a razorblade. Highlights and reflections were similarly scraped out.

This is a successful combination of markers and coloured pencils (right). These media are often used together, as the marker makes a good underlayer for working over with the more opaque medium.

Markers are perfect for quick sketches like this (below). You can suggest an idea very economically and engage the viewer's imagination.

outline underneath, provided it is strong enough to show through, but they will not withstand heavy overworking. If you contemplate much masking out you should choose a substantial support.

Markers are usually thought of as being only suitable for large-scale work to give broad, rapid effects, but detail can be put in with gouache or coloured pencil - it is rare to use markers entirely on their own.

Each stroke of the pen dries with a defined boundary, so to render large areas evenly you must work fast, slightly overlapping each stroke to maintain a wet edge. The more absorbent the support, the more difficult this is. A hard surface such as a line board, where the colour stays wet on the surface, makes it easier for the strokes to blend. You can also use colourless blending markers, which contain solvent. Work some ink from a marker onto a non-absorbent palette, take it up on the blender point and transfer it to the drawing, in gradually decreasing amounts if you want to produce a graded effect. For very even tones you can wipe off ink onto a tissue or cotton wool and spread it on the surface. Moistening with solvent will help.

If you need to produce high-definition work you will have to use masking film. Without it you will find it impossible to produce even colour, because of the blending problems. Each time you stop at the end of a stroke the marker deposits more ink, leaving an intensified mark. With masking you can carry the line over the masked edge. When the mask is removed you will find a clean edge, but it will be slightly fuzzy, because whatever you do the colour bleeds slightly under the edge of the film. You can accept this as being a feature of the medium, and work to a large scale so that on reduction this effect is lost, or you can true up the edges with a positive ink or pencil line, or with bleed-proof white. In rapid sketch

drawings this will not be necessary because the type of illustration and the medium are perfectly matched. If you do need to use bleed-proof white anywhere, note that it will not accept marker ink subsequently applied.

The translucency of the ink means that you can overwork areas to deepen the tone. It is best to wait until the ink is quite dry between applications to obtain maximum strength. Leave the white of the support to play its part, just as you would in a watercolour rendering. Do not use greys to obtain darker tones - in shadows, for example - they will degrade the colour. Select colours of

This project was first drawn in ink line on the reverse side of bleed-proof marker paper. The colour was applied on the back with the help of a light table, and turned over. The marker colours, much modified, show through on the right side.

A fixative was sprayed on this combined water-based and spirit-based marker drawing. The fixative reacts with the spirit-based ink to give unusual and unpredictable mottled effects.

deepening tonal values which work well together. This will maintain clarity. Cutting back different tones to soften and unify them can be done with talcum powder. This also reduces the stickiness that occurs when the support has been overloaded with marker ink.

Always keep your worn-out markers for a time; they may contain just enough ink to give very light controllable tones. An alternative is to use dry pastel washes – they are visually quite compatible with the marker ink. If you are aiming for subtlety of tone and colour you can work in reverse on the back of a thin support. The colour is changed completely when you turn the paper over, and some colours may not show through at all, so you need to experiment in advance. If you decide to prepare your drawing in ink line and to fill in with marker, make sure that the ink will not be dissolved by the solvent and that the line work is quite dry before you start.

A useful technique for obtaining mottled textured effects is to spray on a solvent, such as lighter fuel or some types of fixative, when the marker is still wet. This works as well when the marker has dried if you have used a hard support, as the pigment remains on the surface. You can also use a solvent to reactivate dried-out markers of the screw-top type. The

colour will not be as strong as in the original, and it may dry streakily, but it will provide some useful tints for a limited period.

Fine detail can be picked out with masking fluid and then rubbed clear in the usual way. On hard supports highlights, reflections, fine lines and textures can be scraped out with a razor blade. If you need to apply very lightly toned detail, such as signwriting or glazing bars, over the marker base, you will have to use

bleed-proof white, either neat or mixed, as any other formulation will not cover adequately.

Corrections are difficult to make because the ink soaks into the support, usually staining it. If you try scratching out, the ink will bleed dramatically on recoating. It is possible to lift off colour with a solvent blender, or by soaking the pigment in solvent and blotting it, but there may be no alternative but to cut out the error and patch the support.

This Moscow project shows a typical application of airbrushing techniques. The sky is a watercolour wash, but both the glass and stone-clad towers are airbrushed as a basis for later application of detail by conventional watercolour techniques.

SPRAY PAINTING

The surface effects of sprayed paint are characteristically different from those of brushed colour, because there is no direct contact with the support as the medium is applied. Spray painting techniques may be a useful addition to your repertoire of skills, particularly if your work typically includes large areas of flat or evenly graded colour, or if you require soft-edged or hazy effects for skies and landscape impressions.

Airbrushing

This is not a medium in itself – airbrushing enables you to apply conventional media in a mechanical way. It is a technique widely used for advertising and technical illustration, and requires a high degree of skill if taken to its full potential; but in the field of architectural rendering it has its limitations.

Airbrushing is an ideal method for representing smooth industrial surfaces such as steel or glass, expanses of uniform materials such as concrete and asphalt, and large areas of sky. There is no other technique that allows you to grade colour so precisely, which makes it particularly useful for describing curved surfaces. As underpainting for building facades or even landscapes, it cannot be faulted. Yet the characteristic even, mechanical tonal quality of airbrushed colour makes it unsuitable for rendering the complex textures of most building projects in a sympathetic way, especially in small-scale work. If you use it in a secondary role as underpainting, most of the detail must be put in by conventional methods, and you must be careful to ensure that your brushwork and the airbrush techniques are visually compatible.

The principle of the airbrush is simple. The medium, which must be of a liquid consistency, is contained in a reservoir either above or underneath the airbrush body. Compressed air is forced through a channel in the airbrush body and passes through the nozzle opening; the medium is released through a separate channel and meets the air supply at the nozzle, where it is atomized into a fine spray by the pressure of the air flow. In the most sophisticated types of airbrush commonly used for graphic work, the supplies of air and medium are separately controlled so that you can vary the spray pattern and the ratio of the paint/air mixture.

The air supply can come from a compressor or from a pressurized

Make sure that your airbrush and paintbrush techniques are visually compatible. In this remarkable illustration, with its wealth of detail, there is no sense of incongruity.

Complex multiple masking was used to build up the various solid and transparent surfaces, the reflections and lighting effects. Airbrushing comes into its own in situations like this. To produce this result with a paintbrush would require enormous skill and a great deal of time.

container, connected to the airbrush by a valve and air hose. The container should be adequate for most architectural projects, though it is a limited supply and you cannot vary the pressure. If you intend to specialize in this technique and use airbrushing extensively, you need a reliable electrically-powered compressor that provides a continuous source of air at controlled pressure.

The main media for airbrushing are watercolour and coloured inks. It is most convenient to use concentrated liquid watercolours, but you can dilute the conventional tube paints to the required consistency. These media are transparent and some colours, being chemical dyes, may be fugitive. Gouache can be used for opaque work, but the paint suspension must be sufficiently fine to pass through the airbrush nozzle - any solids quickly block the delicate mechanism. You can also use acrylics, but as they dry so quickly there is a higher risk of blockage. It is vital that the interior of the airbrush is kept free of any dried pigment, so it must be thoroughly flushed out with clean water after use.

To control the spread of colour and create hard-edged shapes, you need to use masking. It may be necessary to go through several masking stages to define the areas you wish to cover, so it is essential to work on a smooth support, which allows masking film to adhere tightly to the surface but also enables you to remove and reapply film as often as is necessary.

You do not always need to use a fixed mask, whether masking film or fluid. For cloud effects, soft landscape profiles, and even outlining your building, a loose mask can be used. This can be a shape torn out of a piece of paper and laid on the surface, or an acetate or card template, which may be held at various distances from the support to vary the edge qualities of the colour area. If you work with the airbrush at differing angles, the spray

Airbrushing is valuable in photo-retouching work because it can provide an even paint surface approximating to the surface quality of the photographic print. In this example the central subject has been overlaid on the photograph using airbrushing for the main surfaces and brushwork for the details.

In this watercolour interior, airbrushing has been used to spray opaque white for reflections and uplighting, to define the ceiling coffers, and for the 'sunburst' points.

the surface, there are no problems with paint pick-up. You can 'knock back' the background to your building with a light overspray, or 'ghost' elements of the structure in cutaway illustrations. You can vignette the illustration so that it floats freely on the support.

For textural detail you can produce a spatter effect by reducing air pressure, or using a spatter cap available for certain airbrush types. Spraying through open-weave fabrics or fine metal mesh can produce interesting textures. A fine pencil eraser will take out highlights in watercolour work, where the pigment is thin, or you can scratch back the paint surface with a scalpel blade on a smooth support, but highlighting for work in gouache or acrylic must be added with opaque white.

This is a technique that has much to offer, particularly in 'broad-brush' effects over which you can add finer detail. However, once you have mastered the technique of using the airbrush – and there are many excellent manuals on the subject – you will find that most of your time is taken up with working out the correct sequence of masking and spraying, and with cutting the masks. Because of this time-consuming, mechanical

will drift under the edge of the loose mask to form a blurred boundary – the further away the mask, the more indefinite will be the image. Try spraying around the edge of cotton wool laid on the surface for detailed cloud forms. Soft masks are also very useful for creating cast shadows with diffused edges.

The masking technique means that you can put in any part of your illustration at any time, provided you can keep control of the picture balance. You could put in the background last, for example, or work from dark to light, even though you may be using a transparent medium. Because the airbrush never touches

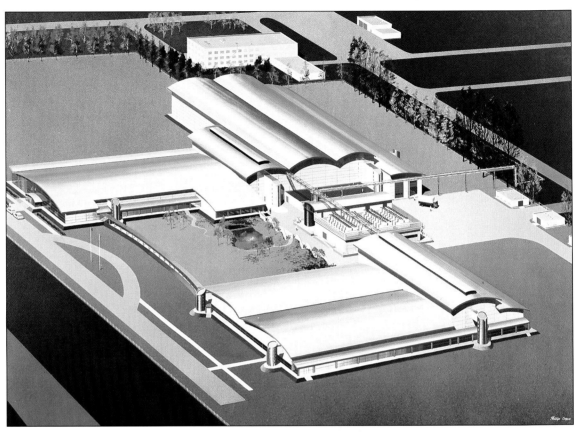

This simplified landscape treatment using cellulose aerosol sprays focuses attention on the building details. Simultaneous spraying with different colours was used to achieve the limited graded effects. Any superimposed detail was painted in gouache. Aerosol sprays are difficult to control, but are quick to use, and are adequate for broad effects like this.

aspect of airbrush work, you should consider whether other techniques might be more appropriate before investing in expensive airbrushing equipment.

Aerosol sprays

Many of these are now CFC-free, so you can use them with a clear conscience, but you need to work in a well-ventilated studio. They are made essentially for vehicle spraying, and dry with a light sheen, which can be reduced with a light overspray of matt white primer. If you do not wish to be involved with airbrush equipment, aerosols are a very good alternative for background work on a large scale, particularly for skies and landscape. There is a vast colour range, and overspraying, or simultaneous spraying, produces subtle effects. The sprayed paint is opaque, and can be overpainted with body colour, although you may need to cut the surface with talc or a hard eraser. The paint dries very rapidly and the main disadvantage is that the spray is rather coarse, and you can get unexpected spattering from pigment blockage.

Pre-printed tones, technical pen and airbrushing are combined in this striking mixed-media study (left) prepared for publicity purposes. The applied colours can be matched exactly to printing inks.

Diffuser sprays

This traditional method of spraying fixative can also be used for spraying a paint medium, usually watercolour. It is very difficult to achieve a uniform coverage, and the spray droplets are very coarse, so they are really only usable for texturing over a washed background, particularly as the results are quite unpredictable.

Spray markers

If you are working with markers, you can use a proprietary system in which

a fine-line marker is attached to a special spray-head unit connected to a compressed air supply. Air is blown over the top of the marker, carrying the marker ink with it as a fine spray. It will only cover small areas evenly, but is adequate for occasional small-scale use.

MIXED MEDIA

Many architectural renderers employ more than one medium in the same illustration - ink line and wash is an

Technical pens, markers, coloured pencils, printed tones and watercolour are used in this mixed-media study for an Italian development. Notice how the line width is constant throughout the drawing.

obvious example - but there are other combinations which can be equally successful. Ink line can be used with marker pen, coloured pencil and airbrushed ink or watercolour; pastel, coloured pencil, ink line and graphite pencil work well together; gouache can be combined with dry pastel wash and coloured pencil. These are only some of the possibilities. Any combination can be used provided that it forms a uniform rendering, and you must choose media which are visually and technically compatible. Pre-printed coloured papers graded from dark to light can form useful skies, which you can work over with body colour, with a great saving in time. Complete illustrations can be built up using pre-printed tones, usually in conjunction with line work. These can be very effective, although time-consuming, and their solid colours reproduce admirably.

Collage techniques can be useful, particularly in illustrating concepts, rather than actual buildings. Here, photographs of building elements, vehicles, or figures taken from your reference sources can be superimposed and worked over with body colour to form a coherent composition. These may not illustrate a project in detail, but will provide the atmosphere which the designer is trying to promote. Collage can be rephotographed and retouched to

produce a striking image. You can incorporate your subject into an existing scene with photomontage techniques. When rephotographed the old and the new should be almost indistinguishable.

You should judge any of these mixed media techniques under two criteria - is the final illustration aesthetically satisfying, and does it communicate your message in the best possible way?

This bold rendering uses ink line drawing as a base for airbrushed watercolour for the main surfaces. Broad detail has been added with markers, and fine detail drawn with coloured pencil, fine-line markers and opaque white drawing ink.

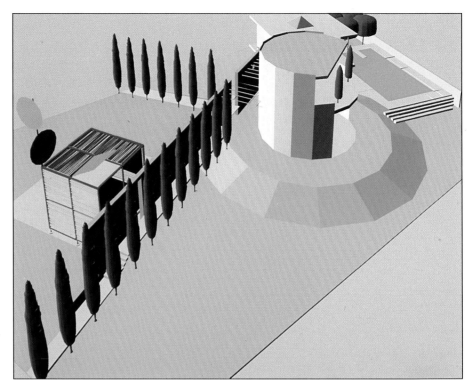

COMPUTER RENDERING

The computer can be used in architectural rendering in three ways. You can use it to generate the perspective framework of the project, which you then illustrate by conventional means. This eliminates the routine task of setting up your perspective, but of course either you or the designer has to spend time entering the basic information into the computer, and it then has to be printed out as hard copy for you to use. Once the data has been entered, the computer can produce as many alternative views as your client could wish for, but the images provide only the bare bones of the project, and you will have to fill in all the detail from the designer's drawings.

The computer can be used as a design tool, exploring alternative aspects of a design while it is being developed, either on screen or in printed form. This usually takes place in the design studio itself, and eliminates the need for concept sketches prepared manually.

You can produce a finished rendering entirely on the computer. In all these processes you are using a machine to produce the impression you are looking for. There is a mechanical interface between you, as artist, and the end product. Many illustrators are not happy with computer work because it removes them from direct contact with the end product, even though the graphic skills required are considerable. You have an infinite choice of viewpoint, lighting conditions, time of day and climate, yet if you wish to show your subject in a natural landscape, with all the incidental detail of the human figure and the products which surround us, there is no doubt that the computer cannot yet match the personal input of the conventional illustrator.

This is a typical sketch-design computer rendering (above) exploring generalized aspects of the proposals as they are developed.

Theoretical work can easily be explored on the computer (left). There are no restrictions on the number of possible views, or the amount of detail which can be added or subtracted.

If you want to render your building with photographic realism, in isolation, it is perfectly possible to do this, as the computer has a limitless facility for sectional enlargement which allows you to put in as much fine detail as you wish for incorporation in the finished artwork. You can also illustrate sequences, moving easily through sites and buildings at any chosen eye level, which in conventional terms would be a hopelessly time-consuming task. The computer is ideal for the representation of theoretical and fantastic architectural concepts, which do not necessarily need realistic detail to get their message across.

The illustrative process itself is relatively straightforward, once the building details have been fed into the computer. With the most advanced systems, work is carried out on a graphics tablet with a stylus, and a

Alterations in time of day or artificial lighting conditions are easily made on the computer (below), once the information relating to each element has been assembled. This can be of great value in the design process.

screen displays all the illustrative options available, usually along the bottom of the screen. The graphics mode enables you to draw lines of various thicknesses and definitions. The painting mode offers options on painting or airbrushing, for example. In either mode the palette of colours can be called up, with thousands of available combinations. Areas of colour can blend into one another, or they can be hard-edged. Any part of the illustration can be called up if you want to make alterations. The final images can easily be produced as permanent colour transparencies. The difficulties of producing hard copy with accurate colour rendering have now been largely overcome.

This apparently simple process can produce images of outstanding virtuosity, but computer images are as open to manipulation as any ordinary perspective. There is some evidence of a resistance to computer renderings submitted in support of building projects because they look too good to be true! So make sure in advance that your efforts are not going to be misplaced. You should also remember that your work is only as permanent as the data storage system which holds it on disc or tape.

STEP-BY-STEP GUIDE

PROJECTS IN PROGRESS

Tempera

John Haycraft

The scale and purpose of this rendering allow the illustrator to take a free, vigorous approach in conveying the mood and character of the project rather than precise architectural detail. A key to the quality of light and atmosphere was taken from the architect's description of the Jakarta sky as 'Turneresque': the artist chose to use a reproduction of J.M.W. Turner's *San Giorgio Maggiore* as reference for the sky colours.

The image is at first loosely worked wet-in-wet with broad washes of tempera; detail is then gradually developed over the translucent underpainting using finer brushwork and introducing areas of opaque colour; in the final stage, pastels provide vivid colour accents. Throughout, a primary concern is to maintain the vitality of the rendering and allow accidental marks and textures to contribute to the overall impression.

Architects Philip Cox, Richardson, Taylor & Partners
Developer Balimata Group

THE BRIEF

A full-colour rendering of a hotel development to show the preliminary design approach, for presentation to the client in Jakarta, Indonesia. A large format was required by the architect commissioning the rendering. The paper size is 763x1017mm (30x40in).

MATERIALS

Tempera
Pastels
Art paper, 140 gsm
Brushes, round sable nos. 3, 6 and 8, 50mm (2in) decorator's brush

I Before beginning the colour rendering, the artist draws up a pencil tonal study, which forms a plan for the painting. The impression is of high-key values with dark accents, using the curved podium to provide a strong lead-in from the left to the centre of interest. The tonal study and a reproduction of the Turner painting used as reference for sky colours are assembled with the line artwork.

2

2 The paper surface is thoroughly wetted with clean water using a 50mm (2in) decorator's brush. The sky is flooded in from the left with dark yellow and a touch of orange, from the right with diluted ultramarine blue. The foreground is treated with the same colours, reversing their positions, with a little spectrum violet added to the blue at the bottom of the paper. The washes are kept very fluid and the board is lifted and tilted to make the colours run where required.

3 The initial underpainting is allowed to dry completely. Colouring of the glazing on the tower begins with free washes laid in over the facade, ignoring the line detail, using a no. 8 brush. The first washes are of orange with burnt sienna, applied heavily at the top of the building and lightened toward the base. A touch of Vandyke brown is added to block in the modelling of the facade, with ultramarine applied to the faces in part-shade. A heavily sedimented wash of Vandyke brown and ultramarine is laid over the shaded side.

3

4 *A dense wash of Vandyke brown and ultramarine with a touch of violet is used to put in reflections on the glass from the structural elements of the facade. Some black is added for the reflections at the bottom of the tower. Detail of the podium is loosely brushed in using the same colour mix.*

5 *A heavy-bodied mix of orange, turquoise blue, burnt sienna, and a touch of white for opacity, is used to pick out the undersides of projecting elements on the tower facade. Dark yellow and more white are added toward the bottom of the tower to indicate light reflecting upward from the top of the podium. Tonal values are strengthened at the top of the tower, drybrushed with Vandyke brown and spectrum violet, to make it read clearly against the sky.*

4

5

6

6 *Using a no. 6 brush, shadowed vertical surfaces in the framework of the facade are delineated with opaque white and burnt sienna, with a touch of Vandyke brown for coolness. The same colour is used for shadows on the sunlit faces where appropriate. Sections in part-sun are brushed in with white and dark yellow modified with yellow ochre.*

7 *The front surfaces of the facade are painted with opaque white warmed with dark yellow. The colour mix is darkened slightly with orange and a touch of mid-brown to model the facade as it turns away from direct sun. The most oblique horizontal faces in full sun are highlighted by applying a pure, clean warm white with a no. 3 brush.*

7

8 The grass in the foreground is laid in with a mixture of olive green, dark yellow and yellow ochre. For the shadows, ultramarine and black are added to the mixture; light yellow is used for highlighting, and a few streaks of pure turquoise blue are added to 'lift' the colours. The road is modelled more heavily with vigorous brushstrokes of ultramarine and violet, with the occasional addition of magenta. This area of the painting is kept loose, with free brushwork broadly defining the planes, directions and shapes.

Some simple reflections of the main building's colours and forms are worked into the pool in the centre of the grassed area.

8

9

9 Details are loosely brushed into the colonnade, aiming for an impression of activity and patterns of light tied together by a strongly expressed built structure. Shadowy recessed areas are enlivened with points of light. The planting around the tower entrance and upper levels of the podium is described with olive green, ultramarine and black, flicking the colour in freely to capitalize on accidental shapes and textures.

The shade side of the tower is picked out of the dark with ultramarine mixed with small touches of Vandyke brown and white. The entrance to the tower and the surrounding canopies are developed in more detail, using high-key colour for the canopies with dark underpinning to obtain crisp contrasts. Rich, warm colours are applied to the entrance – light red, dark red, burnt sienna and white – to attract attention to this focal point of the rendering, and primary reds are also used on the entry steps to draw in the viewer.

10 The tree shapes are brushed in with a mixture of olive green, ultramarine and black. Brighter colours in the planting are added using olive and light greens with light yellow, laid in heavy impasto marks.

The cars are modelled by painting in the shadows and leaving the colours of the underpainting to show through. Pure white highlights are applied to suggest glints from the glass and metal surfaces; for the car on the left, in shade, a touch of ultramarine is added.

The final detail in the foreground is the line of flagpoles on the grassed area. Care is taken to ensure that they are absolutely vertical and straight.

10

11 Colour accents are dashed in using pastels, highlighting existing shapes and adding an impressionistic effect of figures walking through the colonnades and entering the hotel. The shapes are imprecise, applied very rapidly and freely to enliven the rendering and enhance the sense of freshness and vitality.

11

Airbrushed gouache

Tim Monk

One of the most appropriate uses of airbrushing in architectural rendering is for the representation of a large expanse of highly reflective glazing. The uniform facade of a glass-walled tower block is an ideal subject for airbrush treatment. The subtle grading of tones in reflected sky colours, for example, is difficult to achieve by any other technique when applied to a relatively large area of the image.

Opaque gouache is used here, in preference to transparent water-colour, to describe both the hazily mirrored surface of the glass and the dense, roughened texture of concrete. As with the majority of airbrush renderings, an important contribution to the finished effect comes from detail and highlighting brush-painted on the sprayed colour areas.

THE BRIEF

The colour rendering is a development of a pencil sketch, required by the architect for a preliminary presentation to the client. The image is designed to represent the general character and architectural style of the proposed project, an office building for an urban site in Kuwait.

MATERIALS

Gouache
Line board
Airbrush
Brushes, round sable nos. I and 2
Masking film
Graphite pencil
Detail paper
Transfer paper

1

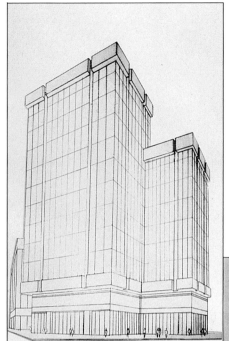

1 The perspective view is drawn up in pencil line on detail paper, for transfer to the illustration board.

2

2 The image is traced down on the board using red transfer paper. The horizontal lines of the glazed panels are drawn over in ink, as they will appear black in the final image.

3

3 The whole image area is covered with masking film. Initially, the mask sections covering the glazed areas are cut and removed in sequence, working from dark to light. To minimize the time and effort required for cutting and removing masks, the full masking sequence is planned ahead. Large areas of colour are to be applied first, to cover the white support completely and obtain a balance of tones. Contrasts can then be enhanced or 'knocked back' to adjust the balance.

4

4 *Reflections of building silhouettes in the lower glazed areas are sprayed with ocean blue, Vandyke brown and black to produce a soft blending of subtle shadow colours. The upper areas of glazing are sprayed with light blue-grey tones representing reflected sky colour. The outline of the shadow area is masked with a piece of tracing paper cut to shape. The tonal depth is built up in repeated sprayings, allowing the colour to dry in between. Paper masks are also used in spraying the dark shadows under the parapet.*

To develop the tonal differences between the highlighted glass on the right-facing planes of the building and the slightly shaded walls angled away from the light source, a sheet of paper is used to mask off the leading edge of the building while the tones are strengthened on the lefthand plane.

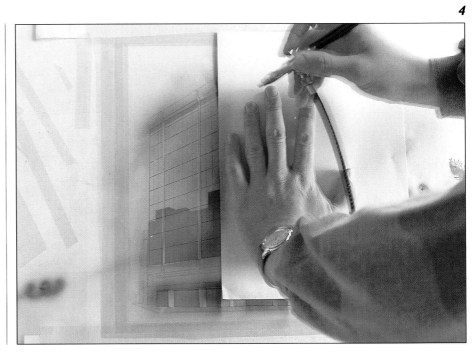

5 *The plans of the building are modelled by spraying more heavily at critical edges and changes of profile, with lighter tones at the back edges suggesting reflected light. A fine layer of white is overlaid on pale-toned areas to reduce the emphasis of the ink line. When colouring of the glazing is complete, the masking film is removed. The image is remasked and the film is cut and peeled away from the areas representing concrete sections of the construction.*

5

6 *The concrete is sprayed in graded tones of mid-brown, following the established pattern of light and shade. The textured finish is simulated by spraying with a spatter cap to create a fine, irregular mottling on the surface.*

6

7 *Further spraying is applied to soften and grey the spattered colour, producing a more uniform but subtly textured surface effect. With all the masking removed, highlights and linear details are hand-painted. The vertical divisions and undersides of the concrete blocks are given hard shadow; lit edges are highlighted with pale yellow-browns and white. The vertical lining of the glazed areas is highlighted with finely painted white lines.*

8 *The buildings and ground plane are masked out and the sky is sprayed with gently variegated tones of ocean blue fading to almost white, suggesting light, soft cloud in an intense blue sky.*

7

9

8

9 *The street surfaces are painted as planes of flat colour, with a mid-toned, hard-edged cast shadow extending from the base of the main building. The background buildings are given strong, dark tone on the vertical surfaces to throw into relief the lower levels of the central subject. To complete the rendering, figures are added in the foreground and trees in the background, and brush-painted detail is applied to enhance contrasts and highlights on the building forms.*

Pencil

John Haycraft

The versatility of graphite pencil and the expressive range of its tones and textures are well represented in this drawing. The direct and lively technique exploits both line and tone to create a substantial impression with plenty of incidental detail. In the early stages, the artist works rapidly over the whole picture area to set the tones, creating a cohesive tonal balance within which individual features can be developed more fully.
Architects The Lend Lease Design Group

THE BRIEF

A perspective of a proposed office building in Sydney, Australia, forming part of the documentation to accompany a tender submission. Since the deadline was immovable and design of the project not finalized, a pencil drawing was decided upon for speed, and also because reproduction could be handled in-house and the illustration could be bound into the report at the last minute.

MATERIALS

Graphite pencils, HB, 2B, 4B
Bond paper
Tracing paper
Sandpaper block
Eraser
Razorblade
Straightedge

1 *The set-up is done by computer, allowing several viewpoints to be supplied to the client. The chosen view is detailed and cleaned up on screen, then printed out in sections at the A4 size accommodated by the printer. The sections are assembled into the complete image, which is printed on bond paper.*

The line layout is squared up on the drawing board and covered with a large sheet of heavy tracing paper. Foreground trees and other prominent landscape features and figures are outlined with a sharp HB pencil. The entire set-up is then traced, stopping the line when it passes behind one of the landscape features previously drawn.

1

2 *With a 2B pencil shaped to a chisel point, the sky is lightly shaded to create a cloud pattern that has a dynamic direction leading to the centre of interest in the drawing. The tonal value of the sky is set to throw the parapet of the building into relief.*

2

3 With the chisel edge of the 2B pencil kept honed on a fine sandpaper block, dark tone is developed in the top sections of the glazing, graded to emphasize the curvature of the building. Dark reflections are drawn on the glass behind the trees and detail of the entrance is developed, including heavy shadows that enhance the depth and silhouetted figures where appropriate.

3

4

4 On the glass at the righthand side of the building, a roughly geometric pattern of shapes is shaded in light and mid-tonal values, representing the reflected forms of the building opposite. This is a way of showing that the new development is adjacent to an existing commercial area (a good selling point for the agents). Lighter areas of shading are added to the glass above the entrance, creating a cloud reflection that highlights the central area of interest.

The trees are modelled in detail, starting with a very black silhouette to the left of the entrance and working towards lighter tones at the front of the building. Firm directional strokes of the pencil are used to structure the shapes and textures in the foliage. The tree trunks are drawn with a range of values according to the background tone, setting light against dark and vice versa.

5

6

5 Landscape details are drawn in using the directions of pencil strokes and ground shadows to lead the eye toward the entrance area. A wet road is described with broad, simple strokes creating subtle reflections of the building and cars. This device helps to emphasize both the height of the building and the landscape detail in the rendering. Cars and people are rapidly described in line and tone, with values creating contrast against the background tones in each case.

Tones are darkened at the top of the building, to enhance the contrast against the sky. A 4B pencil is additionally used to give more depth to the blacks.

6 The drawing is lightly sprayed with fixative and an eraser is used with an eraser shield to clean up edges where strokes have overrun and spoiled the crispness. After another coat of fixative, the framework of the glazing in the curtain wall is scratched out using a razorblade guided against a straightedge. This technique requires practice to get the correct angle and tension on the tip of the blade, to avoid making blurred, scraped lines if the blade is too flat, or cuts in the drawing if the blade angle is too sharp.

Watercolour

David Purser

This rendering shows the potential redevelopment of a site in Coventry, England, currently occupied by a nineteenth century warehouse building in traditional style constructed in red brick and with metal window frames. The project illustrated is an imposing new building designated as office space, initially proposed as suitable for occupation by a single large institution or company. The new building, which will completely replace the old warehouse, is designed to appear sympathetic to its immediate surroundings and to the general character of the location.

Translucent watercolour washes give clarity and freshness to the image. Crisp definition of hard edges and linear frameworks is achieved with ink line and opaque white highlighting applied with a ruling pen.

Architect Andrews Sherlock & Partners

Client Metropolitan and Suburban Properties Ltd.

THE BRIEF

With an initial direction as to the angle of view required by the client, the artist selected a viewpoint that would provide the overall impression of the whole building, with focus on a main entrance area. Road and pedestrian traffic are included to indicate the general context of activity in and around the site. As shown in step 3, a partially coloured print of the detailed perspective drawing formed the basis for further discussion with the client on how the colour rendering would convey the specific qualities of materials and finishes.

MATERIALS

Watercolour tube paints
White gouache
Arches not (cold-pressed) watercolour paper
Tracing paper
Graphite pencils, 7H and F
Brushes; round sable no. 10 and synthetic no. 4
Technical pens, nib sizes 0.2 and 0.1
Ruling pen
Sponges
White wax candle

I

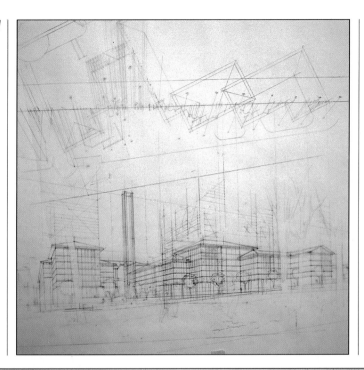

I The perspective is set up in the conventional way by projecting from the architect's plan. The plan is placed on the drawing board at approximately the angle of view suggested by the client, sight lines are taken, and the drawing angle is adjusted to give the best view of the various elements of the building.

2 The drawing is projected on tracing paper a size that fits comfortably on the drawing board area. The tracing is prepared for transfer by rubbing graphite dust, taken from a pencil sharpener, across the back of the tracing paper. The tracing is positioned on the board over the sheet of watercolour paper and traced down using a 7H pencil.

The traced-down image is cleaned up with a putty rubber and the lines are drawn over with an F pencil.

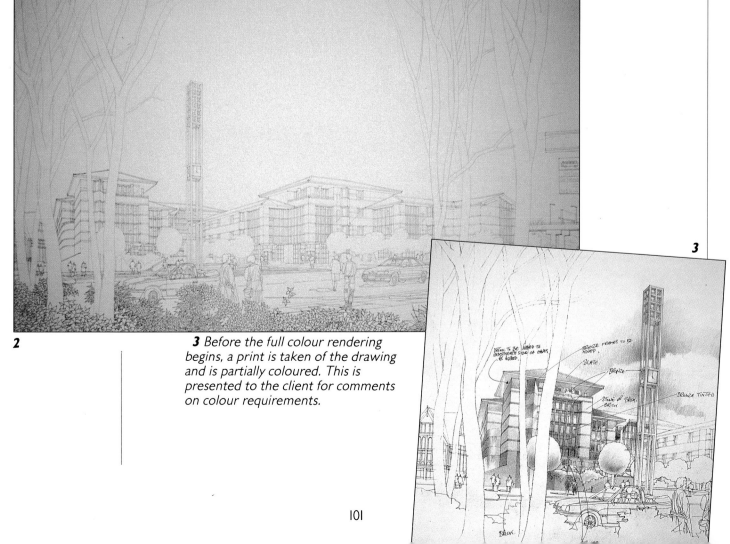

2

3

3 Before the full colour rendering begins, a print is taken of the drawing and is partially coloured. This is presented to the client for comments on colour requirements.

4

4 *The sky is painted first, using free washes of colour to create the cloud effects more or less at random. The paper surface is soaked with clean water and the colours are flooded in with a no. 10 sable brush – Winsor blue and ultramarine, with touches of Naples yellow in the clouds. The washes are taken down over the tree trunks and sections of the building that project into the sky area, to avoid the need to cut in accurately to specific shapes and hard edges, which would inhibit the flowing application of the washes. The excess paint is subsequently lifted from areas where it is not required while still wet.*

Sky colours are introduced to the windows of the building and cars, and the roofs are painted in tonally as hard-edged shapes using Payne's grey and neutral tint.

5

6

5 *When the initial washes applied to the windows are dry, these areas are repainted in more detail with the no. 4 brush to introduce shadows, the colours of tinted glass as specified, and darker ground reflections. The delicate areas of wash representing these elements are overpainted on the reflected sky colours quite precisely, using raw sienna, burnt sienna and alizarin crimson.*

6 *The light tone of the stonework is applied with Naples yellow and raw sienna, using drybrush technique to suggest the surface texture of the stone. Cast shadows are developed by darkening the colours with slight additions of ultramarine and neutral tint. The structural detail of stonework and window frames is also carefully delineated with darker tones, introducing Vandyke brown and burnt sienna to the colour mixes.*

7

7 The brickwork at the base of the building is painted following the overall pattern of light and shade already established on the vertical surfaces. The warm colours of the brick derive from adding burnt sienna and brown madder to the colour range, with the darker-toned shadows again strengthened with neutral tint and ultramarine.

At each stage as colours are added, the edges of the shapes are cleared of darker 'tide marks' by wetting small areas with clean water and lifting the excess colour with clean white blotting paper.

The detail of the window frames is emphasized by using a ruling pen and white gouache to apply highlighting.

8 Initial colour washes are applied to the clock tower, roads and paved areas, first using Naples yellow, then toning with neutral tint, Payne's grey and burnt sienna. With the board turned so that the righthand side is at the top, a very wet wash is run into the roadway, beginning with Payne's grey and sky blue and merging in warmer tones of siennas and Vandyke brown in the area closest to the observer.

When the washes have dried, shadows are emphasized with stronger tones of the colours previously used, and the street signs at right are painted in detail.

8

9

9 The linear structure of the clock tower is redefined using a technical pen to sharpen the edges and a ruling pen and white gouache to add highlighting. This kind of detail is introduced at various stages throughout the painting process: it is necessary to be very careful when laying in washes after opaque white has been applied, as the white can easily bleed into surrounding colours if wetted and dragged with the brush.

Sap green modified with Vandyke brown, ultramarine and burnt sienna is used to wash in the background landscape and the general shapes of trees and shrubs in the middle ground and foreground.

10 *After allowing all the colour washes to dry, foreground details are developed with stronger colours. Each of the cars is given its individual colour - bronze, dark red and blue - and a pattern of reflected colour. Details such as windshields and wheels are defined with technical pen and ruling pen.*

The figures in the foreground are similarly described with line and colour, and developed three-dimensionally with details such as folds in the clothing; the figures further away from the viewer, are given more generalized shapes.

Individual leaf shapes are drawn into the foreground foliage and surrounded with intricate shadows

11 *A technical pen is used to delineate the trunks and branches of the large foreground trees and the smaller trees in front of the building. The foliage is given greater detail and density of colour and texture, using a natural sponge soaked in wet paint to dab colour on to the support. The varying tones are built up light to dark; the first colour application is allowed to dry, then a darker tone is dabbed on, and so on until the required tonal range is achieved.*

A hairdryer can be used to speed up this process, but it needs careful handling when there are wet pools of colour lying on the paper's surface; the jet of hot air can blow the wet paint into awkward shapes, and if dried too quickly the shapes develop dark outlines where a colour build-up accumulated at the edge of the washes.

11

13

13 The dark colours of the trunks are washed in with mixtures of sap green, Vandyke brown and ultramarine. As the watery paint is repelled by the wax, a rough texture automatically develops. The colour is brushed in evenly over the areas of cast shadow on branches and trunks which have been left free of wax.

12 After all the detail of trees and shrubs in the middle ground and upper part of the rendering has been brought to the appropriate degree of finish, all that remains is to complete the painting of the foreground trees. A wax resist technique is used to create the bark texture on the thick tree trunks. Wax from an ordinary domestic candle is applied to the areas of the tree trunks that catch the light.

12

14 In the finished rendering the building is effectively framed by the arrangement of the foreground planting. The balance of colour and tone enhances the depth of the perspective view. The detail picture shows how careful attention to the individual elements of cast shadows, highlights and reflected colours gives vitality to the depiction of the building's structure and surface finishes.

Coloured pencil

John Deputy with Frank Costantino

This demonstration shows a now widely used application of the versatile medium of wax-based coloured pencils. The pencils are applied to front and back of translucent drafting film, a technique that allows a complex layering of colours with subtle modulations of hue and tone. The result is a vibrant image admirably suited to any promotional uses associated with a building project.

The colour drawing is based on a previously completed graphite pencil rendering and illustrates only a third of the residential building complex. Initial selection of the colour palette was derived from the colours of the building materials and the coastal marsh environment of the site. The specific pencils to be used were tested in a partial study prior to the final application. The visual effect intended for the completed artwork was a bright summer's day in a scenic seashore location.

Architect Ahearn/Schopfer Associates, Architects

THE BRIEF

A demonstration colour study of the building proposal for Red Lion Residences, Provincetown, Massachusetts, showing part of the building with an indication of its landscape surroundings.

MATERIALS

Wax-based coloured pencils
Drafting film
Tracing paper
Masking tape

1

1 *The detail area forming the composition for this rendering is outlined on a line layout of the original perspective. Shade and shadow projections are blocked in with a red pencil.*

2

2 *A line tracing of the image is transferred to drafting film, using a light table to give a clear view of the base artwork through the translucent film. The line of the background trees is altered to adjust the balance of the composition.*

3

3 *The first colouring stage is applied to the back of the drafting film. The sky and window reflections are shaded with light blue, grading the tones to create an impression of soft clouds. The water is coloured with aquamarine blue.*

4 *Still working on the reverse of the support, all the shade and shadow areas on the building are coloured with ultramarine blue. To suggest an effect of reflected ground light, the lower parts of the building faces are graded to a lighter value. These base colours are applied quite strongly to the back of the film; from the right side they appear more muted and the intensity can be controlled by the colour layers applied from the front.*

4

5

5 *On the front of the film, the initial tone of the shingle colour on the building is applied with raw umber to the lit surfaces and some shaded areas. Note that the perimeter of the drawing is masked with tape to ensure a clean edge on the finished image.*

6 *The landscape surrounding the building is worked on both sides of the film. The foliage is shaded in marine green (right), with olive green blended into the lower portion of the trees behind the building, to give stronger definition to that edge and to highlight the top edge of the foliage area below. The grass in the foreground is built up on the right side of the film (far right) using layered strokes of raw umber and sepia over a sand yellow base.*

6

7

8

7 The full area of marsh grass is completed, varying the density of the pencil strokes to grade the colours and tones across the ground area. A decision is made not to include the overlapping foliage shapes at the lefthand corner, as originally depicted in the line drawing. Still working from the front of the drawing, the building colours are further shaded with raw umber and sepia.

8 Cool colour is added to the shaded surfaces of the building's white trim using light blue applied to the reverse of the support, with the pencil point blunted to obtain smooth, non-linear coverage. The darker recesses of the shaded interior spaces are suggested by the use of dark warm grey in the window areas, following a preplanned pattern of tonal values designed to give a lively contrast of darks and lights on the glass panes. The tower windows are rendered with a transparent effect achieved by shading in the darkened planes of the interior walls and showing their windows in pale tone.

The small area of vertical retaining wall below the foliage on the left is lighly covered with raw umber and sand yellow.

9

11

11 To relieve the rather flat effect of the textured grass surface, some of the colour is removed with a kneaded eraser, adding visual interest to the foreground and suggesting highlights and movement.

12

9 At this stage of the drawing, some adjustments are made to the tonal and colour balance of the image. The upper sky at the edge of the picture is deepened in hue with applications of light blue and mid-blue. The recessed area of the retaining wall is softened with sepia and indigo blue. From this point, with the main elements of the image established, the illustrator becomes concerned with many minor decisions on hue, value, contrast and texture that contribute the sparkle of detail and final enhancing touches.

10 Foreground detail of a shrub and tall grasses is reworked on a separate overlay and rendered into the main image. Trees in the mid-section and background of the image are enriched with yellow, olive and marine greens, with indigo and black used to darken the shadowed wall-shrub.

12 The marsh grass is further defined by applying colour to both front and reverse of the support, using sand yellow, sepia and raw umber. Light colour mixes are applied to the reverse, in the most distant parts of the grass area, and darker hues are built up on the front of the drawing in the foreground, to create a convincing depth of field.

10

13 To differentiate shade and cast shadow on the white trim surfaces, the shadows are strengthened with a mixture of light violet and light blue. To enhance the contrasts where needed, light blue is added to the shade areas on the front, where the same colour has already been applied to the reverse, and darker tones are emphasized with indigo blue and raw umber.

13

14

14 Indigo blue is sparingly stroked into the window areas, to suggest the reflectivity of the glass and soften the contrast of the black colouring.

15

15 Light violet is more strongly applied to the shadows on the white trim to define the edges between shadows and lit surfaces. Similarly, graded values are applied in the foreground stream using light, mid and aquamarine blues, to enhance the effect of depth. Reflections of the grass are added with raw umber and aquamarine blue.

16

16 The drawing is completed with a number of finishing touches, including detail enhancement, some erasure on front and back of the support, and redefinition of lost lines.

Watercolour

Mark Wearne

The restaurant depicted in this rendering, called 'Paganini', has a loose musical theme and the room is decorated with carved mahogany panels and rich, bold patterns. The design is intended to create an exclusive but relaxed atmosphere that needs to be conveyed in a rendering of sophisticated style and finish.

For this reason a detailed treatment of the interior and fixtures is proposed, painted in watercolour which allows great subtleties of colour, tone and detail. The artist makes full use of watercolour's delicate, translucent texture to translate the discreet light effects that play across the room, using premixed colour washes that provide a subtly graded range of warm and cool colours.

Designers David Hicks International

THE BRIEF

A visual of a brasserie-style restaurant as part of a presentation showing proposals for interior refurbishment of a luxury hotel. Plans, elevations and finishes were supplied by the designers.

Figures are to be included in the drawing to give scale and purpose to the space, but without making the image too crowded or busy. Lighting is mainly downlighting from central pendant fittings, but there are also windows along one wall of the restaurant providing a natural light source.

MATERIALS

Watercolour tube paints
Watercolour board, 'not' (cold-pressed) surface
Brushes, round synthetic nos. 5, 7 and 10; flat synthetic 3mm, round squirrel hair no. 12
Airbrush
Opaque white
White ink
Layout paper
Graphite stick
Fine ballpoint pen
Graphite pencil, HB

1

1 A viewpoint for the rendering is chosen to portray the scale of the large room and also to provide interesting detail in the foreground that will draw the viewer into the image. From this spectator point, the entrance area is visible in the middle distance and the restaurant bar creates a strong background to the view across the room.

The perspective framework of the room setting is drawn up as a pencil layout and figures are roughly located representing diners and restaurant staff.

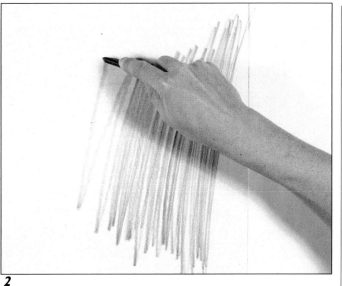

2

2 In preparation for transferring the drawing to the final support, a graphite stick is used to cover the back of the layout paper with a scribbled layer of graphite.

3

3 *The layout paper is placed over the watercolour board and the image is traced down using a fine ballpoint pen. Once the main framework of the image is traced, the layout paper is removed and detail of the drawing is developed on the board using an HB pencil. Erasures are kept to a minimum at this stage, to avoid damage to the board surface.*

4

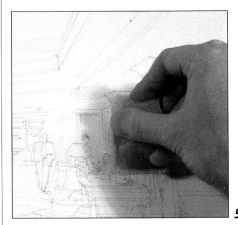

5

4 *This picture represents a stage of drawing together all the necessary information before colouring of the image begins. The factors to be considered are the quality of lighting and atmosphere of the restaurant space; the colour balance of the rendering, established from the samples of finishes supplied by the designer and cross-referenced to magazine pictures of similarly styled interiors; the palette for the work, involving preliminary colour mixing of watercolour washes; and the 'edge qualities' that will frame the image.*

The artist decides to create two hard edges (right side and bottom) and leave two sides fading off (top and left side), so that the illustration can be presented without a mount.

5 *Before any colour is laid, the entire board surface is wetted with clean water until it is evenly saturated and receptive to the colour washes.*

6 *Basic tones and colours are washed in on the wet surface, using the round squirrel brush, which is absorbent and holds plenty of colour. Initially the washes are simple colour areas establishing the quality of light – warm colours on the side of the room lit artificially and cooler shades to imply reflected daylight on the opposite side.*

6

7

7 *The colours are allowed to blend and dry on the board. As the tones lighten during the drying process, further colour washes are needed to enhance the colour and tonal values. The surface of the image is rewetted and darker washes are laid in following a general pattern of light and shade overall. The colours are developed with premixed washes using various mixtures of Winsor blue,* *burnt sienna, yellow ochre, alizarin crimson and neutral tint to develop the warm/cool range.*

Near-saturated colour in the foreground provides a tonal key for the progress of the work. Dark tones are laid into the shapes quite precisely, but with the paler washes the outlines can be ignored as colour to be subsequently overlaid will develop volume and detail.

8 The brushwork now becomes crisper to delineate form and pattern more clearly, and the colour and tonal ranges are developed more broadly. Contrasts of light and shade describing the volume of walls and interior fixtures are made more emphatic. The washes on the vertical surfaces are given slanted variations of tone to imply reflective surfaces.

    The pattern of the carpeting on the floor is painted in detail, using both colour washes and line work delicately drawn in colour with the smaller synthetic hair brushes. Careful attention is given to the way the carpet pattern relates to the perspective of the floor. Colours are modified to represent lit areas and cast shadows from tables and chairs.

8

9

9 The chairs and tables are painted in detail using burnt sienna and brown madder modified with neutral tint and burnt umber to create the mahogany effect. This colouring begins to dominate the image and areas that previously seemed very dark are now evenly balanced across the composition. The wash of Payne's grey on the figure at the left introduces a bluish contrast to the warm colours that keys in further development of the colour range.

10

10 *Each of the figures is given form and volume with additional colour washes, varying from yellow and red hues to cool greys and blues to create subtle points of harmony and contrast against the room colours. Detail on the figures is kept to a minimum, but those in the foreground are slightly more descriptive than the figures at the back of the room, a device that helps to suggest the receding space between them.*

As the colours dry, the contours of the colour-washed areas that form the framework of the room are redefined using a straight-edge to guide the brush.

11 *The airbrush is used to lay a fine layer of spray colour simulating the sheen of the bronze glass sheets that flank the mahogany panels. The airbrushing lays a thin film of gold and brown tones defining the surface plane of the glass, through which the previously rendered detail remains fully visible.*

11

12 *Opaque white tinted with the mahogany colour mixes is used discreetly to bring up the highlighting on the chairs. Small brushstrokes create slashes of crisp, pale tone that give further definition to the shapes. The final touch is the highlighting of the glasses on the tables, tiny bursts of light finely drawn with white ink to give a sparkling finish.*

12

Ink line and airbrushed watercolour

Suns Hung

This rendering features the impressive scale of the proposed Messeturm office building, in Frankfurt, Germany, and also conveys most effectively the complex surface qualities of the granite and glass construction. The distribution of light and shade contributes to varied graphic detail in the rendering of the facade. The glazing in the lower part of the building is shown as primarily transparent, giving access to the interior spaces, while the reflective nature of the glass is emphasized toward the top of the building, with reflected colour from the sky.

The combination of crisp pen and ink drawing with subtly airbrushed tone and colour and hand-painted detail produces an extremely articulate image with an almost photographic intensity. The smooth, flawless surface coverage obtainable with the airbrush is used to good effect in rendering the sky, the facade, and the heavy foreground shadow that helps to suppress distracting detail. The characteristic uniformity of airbrushed colour is enlivened by the freer application of hand-painted highlights and colour accents in transparent watercolour and opaque gouache.

Architect Murphy/Jahn Architect
Client Visual Advertising Services, Inc.

THE BRIEF

A full-colouring rendering for publication in a brochure, describing the tower building in the context of its location and showing the character of the street-level spaces as seen from the plaza. The viewpoint was chosen to supersede an existing rendering, which seemed to be distorted, and to emphasize the tower and plaza. A morning sun angle was chosen which provides the useful compositional device of a large shadow cast by the building in the right foreground.

A preliminary study of tonal values (step 3) demonstrates the artist's intention to dramatize the shape of the tower against a dark sky background. At the client's specific request, for the colour rendering the sky tones were lightened and soft impressions of clouds were introduced.

MATERIALS

Watercolour tube paints
Gouache
Graphite pencil
Illustration board, double-thickness not (cold-pressed) surface
Technical pen

Brushes; round sable and Chinese paintbrush
Airbrush
Masking film

1

I A preliminary pencil layout is chosen from several massing sketches drawn from the architectural blueprint. This drawing establishes the general shape and structure of the tower and its relationship to surrounding buildings in the required perspective view.

2

3

2 A freehand pencil study is drawn up to show the view in more detail and convey the atmosphere of the project and its location. The grid pattern of the building's facade is indicated, and an impression of the activity at ground level, including the tree planting around the tower and pedestrian traffic on the plaza.

3 The next stage is a study of tonal values fully rendered in pencil on heavily grained white paper. The pattern of light and shade on the building is plotted according to the sun angle, emphasizing the three-dimensional projection of the facade and throwing the tower into sharp relief against the sky. The positioning of trees and figures is redefined, opening up the view to the tower base.

4 A more detailed layout of the chosen view is constructed in pencil line, working out the complex grid pattern of the tower building's facade and the architectural frameworks of surrounding buildings.

5 The drawing is transferred to illustration board and rendered in ink line using a technical pen, which provides the necessary line consistency to achieve the intricate formal detail of the building facade. The entourage, trees and figures are drawn with equivalent detail appropriate to the scale.

6

6 The ink drawing is completely covered with masking film and sections of the mask are carefully cut and removed to expose the grid structure of the facade. This is airbrushed with watercolour in delicately graded tones, beginning with sepia shadowing which is oversprayed with Indian red to create the main colour emphasis. The framework is enhanced with touches of dark grey and purple.

The sequence of mask-cutting and spraying continues with monochrome tonal gradation applied to the background buildings, the trees and figures.

7

7 Masking film is reapplied to the complete image to begin work on the glazed sections of the facade. Smoothly graded tones in the illuminated areas and the irregularly edged, heavy shadows on the glass in the lower part of the tower suggest the reflective quality of the surface. As the tonal range develops, further spraying is applied to the surrounding buildings, keeping to the monochrome scheme that gives prominence to the colour treatment of the tower.

9 A mid-toned grey is lightly sprayed over the trees in the right foreground to give density to the forms. The shadowing of the foreground is established with an even grey tone across the ground plane. This is offset by the clarity of the pale green wash laid across the line of trees in the background, which stand in full daylight, and the contrast of light and shade is further emphasized by touches of clear colour brushed into the more distant figures.

9

8

8 In the third stage of masking and spraying, the whole area of sky is completed. The subtle gradations of tone and colour typical of airbrushing are employed to build up the strong blue sky at the top of the rendering, fading into paler, warmer tones toward the horizon. Suggestions of light cloud are oversprayed with opaque white.

10

11

10 Detailed brushwork is applied to the building facade to develop a 'see-through' effect on the glazed areas, giving access to the interior spaces. Dark-toned elements, including silhouetted figures seen through the windows, are applied in watercolour. Bright colour accents that enhance the impression of depth between the reflective glass and the shadowy interiors are overlaid with opaque gouache. Opaque colour is also used to add linear detail to the building's exterior, with white highlighting subtly shaded into pale grey tones emphasizing the structural framework.

Further colour detail is added to the figures and trees at the front of the building, also using the combination of translucent watercolour to define particular shapes and solid gouache to touch in highlights and colour accents.

11 In the finished rendering, the subject building dominates the image because of its central position and its height compared to adjacent buildings, and is emphasized as the focal point by the detailed colour treatment set against the low-key greys of the entourage.

The detail pictures show how effectively the character of the building is investigated by means of the viewpoint angle and distribution of light and shade. The sunlit top of the tower presents the glazed surfaces as blankly reflective, while at the shadowed base of the building, closer to the viewer's eye level, the glazing becomes translucent to convey a sense of the interior spaces and the activity within.

Coloured pencil

Octavio Balda

The main sequence shown here is the process of preparing a coloured pencil rendering of the front view of an office building complex in Hamburg, Germany. The columns at ground floor level give access for vehicles on the left side; an additional parking facility is shown on the right. The composition includes existing details of this site, but omits an unattractive building on the adjacent site, replacing it with the less distracting feature of a long, high wall extending to the left of the subject building.

The technique, a variation of the 'value delineation system' devised by Paul Stevenson Oles, involves producing a detailed monochrome rendering, which is then photographed and the colour work is applied to a photographic print. The translucent quality of wax-based coloured pencils produces an effective synthesis of monochrome and colour detail.

Architect P.A.I., Hamburg

THE BRIEF

Colour renderings of front and back views (see also step 13) of the office building complex, for display to the owners and other interested parties at meetings relating to development of the project and planning applications. The two views also provide the opportunity for the effect of different types of glazing to be compared through alternative colour treatments in the renderings.

MATERIALS

Wax-based coloured pencils
Graphite pencil, 2H
Illustration board, rough surface
Technical pen, nib size 0.13
Airbrush
Spray colour, sapphire blue
Masking film
Putty eraser
Hard eraser
Ellipse templates
French curves

1 A computer plot is made of the structure from the proposed angle of view. This is sent to the architect for approval.

2 The perspective is developed according to the topography of the site — a long curved road which is accentuated by the curve of the building facade. The lamp standard on the left, the trees, the parking lot on the right and the factory building partially shown are all existing elements of the site and its surroundings. These elements are constructed with the aid of computer graphic facilities and photographic techniques. The line layout is drawn in graphite pencil.

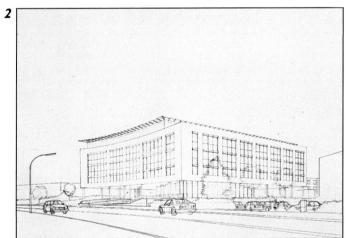

3 The tone and texture of the glazing on the front of the building is laid in, alternating soft drawing with a sharp wax-based black pencil and use of a putty eraser to grade the tones, suggesting sky reflected on tinted glass. Light effects derive from a high sun angle, with the sun positioned almost vertically above the building.

The pattern of brick joints on the facade is scored into the surface of the board. The brickwork is then shaded in using a very dull pencil point, so that the scored lines stand out white against the textured black.

4 *The same techniques are applied to the right side of the building, working carefully around the forms of the trees. Solid dark shading is applied to the undersides of the concrete lintels above the windows and to the vertical edges of the brickwork surrounding the glazing. The metal framework of the glazed panels is accentuated with ink line drawn with the technical pen.*

Part of the planting at the corner of the building is given tone and texture with the black pencil. This provides a tonal key for the dense texture now applied to the asphalt road surface. The white line in the centre of the road is covered with masking tape, then the texture of the road surface is developed, beginning by working over the road area with a dull pencil point which is then progressively sharpened to build up the density of tone.

4

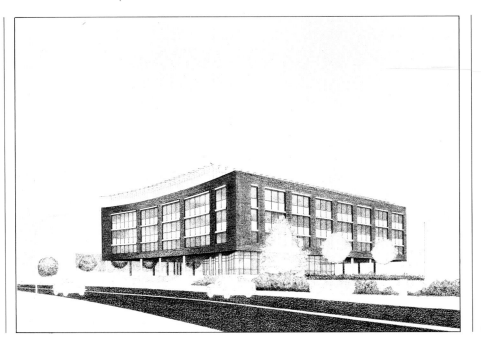

5

5 *Still working with the black pencil only, the glazing at ground floor level is filled in using the same technique as in step 3, but keeping the tones much lighter to give the sensation that the building is suspended. The impression of transparency in the glass at the back end of the right side of the building dramatizes the effect. The* glass facade at the front entrance is in a shaded area and is left almost white, like a mirror. In reality, the ceiling would reflect along the curved facade, but this is omitted to show the entrance area more clearly.

The planting on the right is extended, and the tonal detail of the background trees is laid in. The columns at the base of the building which stand in the shadowed areas are heavily defined with black pencil shading.

6 *The trees and planting on both sides of the building are completed. The glazing on the top floor is described with graded tones, as before, then the interior framework of the steel roof is defined by line work with the technical pen.*

The side of the factory building at right is darkly textured with a dulled pencil point. The building in the far background is laid in with lighter, less distinct tones, as is the long, high wall seen behind the subject building on the left, which is subtly shaded using a medium-sharp pencil point.

The next stage is to detail the cars; those in the parking lot are shaded with light and mid-tones, with some darker ground shadow. The cars on the road closer to the viewer are drawn in graded tones to emphasize the forms, with heavy cast shadows on the road surface beneath. They are treated with the same degree of detail as applied to the building, to maintain the visual balance of the composition.

6

7

7 *The completed monochrome drawing is photographed and printed on a slightly rough-surfaced photographic paper suitable as a support for coloured pencil work. The whole image is covered with masking film, which is cut along the main outlines of the wall, buildings and lamp standard.*

The masking film is peeled away from the sky area. This is airbrushed with a strong tone of sapphire blue, *lightly graded toward the horizon line. An unexpected visual problem occurs here when the paper surface causes linear marks to appear in the airbrushed colour. To avoid beginning the process again, with a tight deadline to meet, the artist decides to disguise the lines by creating more complex cloud effects than originally planned.*

8 The soft, broken cloud cover is developed using a hard eraser to lift the airbrushed colour. This 'negative' drawing method can be carefully controlled to create delicately varied effects of tone and texture. Alternatively, the cloud effects could be airbrushed in opaque white over the blue.

9 With all the masking film removed, colour detail is applied to the building and its surroundings using wax-based coloured pencils. In the first colouring stage, terracotta is applied to the building facade, and the trees and planted areas are developed in olive green, shading with the pencil in a way that creates subtle variations of colour intensity corresponding to the depth and detail of the monochrome drawing.

10 Using the same colours, brickwork on the right side of the building is completed and the planted areas are coloured across the whole width of the image.

At this stage the linear frameworks of windows and roof are redrawn with the technical pen, enhancing the definition of the rendering.

11 *Colour detail is applied to the cars — canary yellow, black and yellow ochre on the lefthand vehicle; cream, black, yellow ochre, scarlet red and white for the central car; dark brown, Copenhagen blue, warm grey and cream for the parked vehicles.*

Sky reflections in the glazing on all levels of the building are coloured with light blue, developing graded tones with pencil shading and eraser as in the monochrome drawing. Cold grey is lightly shaded into the road surface, sidewalk and background wall.

12 *The factory wall at right is coloured with sepia, the background buildings with sepia and terracotta, keeping to low-key mid-tones that are distanced from the stronger colours of the main building. This completes the colour rendering.*

13 *This rendering of the back view of the building demonstrates the advantages of working on photographic paper. A print of the monochrome image again provides the detail, and the point of this rendering was to try out, at the architect's request, the effect of glass tinted in a light 'champagne' yellow with bronze hues. After viewing this version, the architect requested that the front facade be shown with very light grey glazing. The renderings thus play an important role in a significant design decision.*

Gouache

Harold R. Roe

The project is a low-rise office building situated in a corporate office park. The opacity and density of gouache colours are fully exploited in this rendering, in both the colour qualities of the finished image and the technique of overpainting one element on another. The step-by-step sequence shows how the image is gradually layered from background to foreground. The whole area of the support is covered in painting the building itself and the ground plane; the trees and vehicles are then superimposed.

The colour intensity available with this medium gives extreme contrast between the light-coloured finish of the building facade and the darkly shadowed foreground, so that although the building is set back in the composition, it immediately draws the attention.

Architect Geddes, Brecher, Qualls, Cunningham, PC, Architects

Client Mobil Research and Development Corporation

THE BRIEF

A monochrome rendering in pen and ink was commissioned at an early design stage of the project. Some months later, the client requested a full-colour illustration of the same view, to be used in intercorporate communications.

MATERIALS

Gouache
Soft pastels, light oxide red and white
Illustration board, heavy weight, not (cold-pressed) surface
Brushes, round sable, nos. 2, 3, 4 and 6
Airbrush

1 With the building and foreground masked out, the sky is airbrushed with a blend of sky blue, indigo, ultramarine and yellow ochre mixed with titanium white. Clouds are added over the airbrushed colour when dry, using soft pastels to develop the irregular, soft-edged forms.

The background trees are painted in dark tones, using permanent green light and chrome oxide green, ultramarine and ivory black.

1

2 The same colour ranges are used to paint the reflected colours of the sky and tree line on the window glass of the main building. The sky tones are subtly graded from each end of the building so that the brightest area of glazing gives emphasis to the main entrance. Light-toned figures are silhouetted on the glass in the darkest sections at ground and first floor level, giving an impression of interior activity.

2

3 The panels and column of the main building, which consist of an epoxy resin aggregate, are solidly blocked in using titanium white mixed with yellow ochre, ultramarine and Vandyke brown.

3

4 The three-dimensional structure of the building facade is modelled by painting in the shade and shadow lines of the columns, panels and window frames. This fine detail work is brush-ruled with the no. 2 brush guided along a straight-edge. Similar detail is added to the entrance area, where the edges of the door frame reflecting on the glass are painted freehand.

4

5

5 The brick base of the building is painted with mixtures of burnt sienna, yellow ochre and alizarin crimson heightened with white. Colour and tonal values are varied to create the impression of the brick and mortar texture.

6

6 The background buildings are painted with the same range of colours applied to the main building (step 3), but with a greater proportion of Vandyke brown and ultramarine to produce the darker tones.

7 When all the detail of the buildings is completed and the paint has dried, the whole shape is again masked out and the sky retouched with the airbrush to develop a greater contrast between the colours of the buildings and sky.

7

8

8 The asphalt of the foreground parking lot area is painted with titanium white mixed with phthalo blue and yellow ochre in the sunlit areas. The values are graded to develop a high contrast where the foreground cloud shadows cut across the brightest areas of sunlit asphalt.

The shadows are brushed in with a mixture of ivory black, ultramarine and alizarin crimson, with a touch of the sunlight colour mix. A slight dragging at the edges of the brushstrokes softens the shapes.

Grassed areas in the foreground and middle ground are treated according to the existing pattern of light and shade, emphasizing the contrast points. Chrome oxide green and permanent green are used with titanium white for the lit tones, and ivory black and ultramarine are mixed with the greens to create the shadow colours.

9 *The trunk and branch structures of the trees across the front of the building are finely drawn with the no. 2 brush. Ivory black is used, modified with ultramarine and Vandyke brown. Touches of white are added as highlighting according to the sun angle.*

9

10

10 *Foliage cover is painted on the first line of trees before the foreground trees are drawn in. Four basic tonal values are applied to the foliage colours, mixed from chrome oxide green, ultramarine and ivory black, with permanent green light, cadmium yellow medium and white. The foliage masses are fanned onto the branch structures using a no. 4 brush. Drybrush technique is used for highlighting.*

As the dark trunks of the foreground trees are painted, they are drybrushed with a mixture of white, neutral grey, Vandyke brown and yellow ochre, to develop the roundness of the forms and the impression of sunlight. Washes of ultramarine mixed with alizarin crimson are used to enhance shadows and shaping.

11 With all the detail of the trees completed, an automobile layout for the foreground parking lot area is drawn on tracing paper and transferred to the painted rendering.

12 The automobile interiors and tyres are blocked in with ivory black. Shadows below the vehicles are painted with a more intense mixture of the colours previously used for ground shadows.

11

13 The automobiles are given individual colours, working from foreground to background using one basic colour at a time to minimize the effort. Colours are kept muted and greyed, to avoid distracting the viewer from focusing on the building, but discreet highlighting is added to give realism to the forms.

13

12

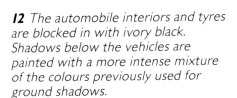

14 In the final stage, figures are painted beside the main entrance, giving further emphasis to the entrance as a focal point of the rendering. The contrast between the dark trees and heavy ground shadows in the foreground and the bright lighting on the building naturally draws the eye into the composition.

14

Ink and watercolour

Don Coe

This is one of a series of renderings illustrating a proposal for restoration and refurbishment of a town centre site in Tunbridge Wells, England. The series was designed to give the viewer an impression of 'walking through' the scheme, to convey the renovation clearly and descriptively to a lay audience. Detailed roughs were prepared, a time-saving process in that all viewpoints could be fixed and approved before final artwork began, with modifications incorporated as necessary, and any problems that occurred in translating to perspective views from the architect's plans could be quickly seen and rectified in the initial stages.

The illustrator's technique and use of materials are standardized so that clients know exactly what to expect and can feel confident of the style and presentation of the finished rendering.

Architect Manning, Clamp & Partners
Client Speyhawk plc, Developers

THE BRIEF

To produce a series of line and wash colour sketches illustrating the restoration proposals. The illustrations were for use in presentations to interested parties during various planning enquiries, and for public exhibition.

At the first briefing, the possible viewpoints and appropriate elevations were discussed with the architect and client. The number of sketches, time schedule and cost of the work were established. The illustrator then prepared simple thumbnail sketches evaluating the content and architectural priorities of each view and establishing some of the compositional devices to be used.

MATERIALS

Watercolours in full pans
Watercolour paper, 140lb, rough surface
Round sable brush no. 8
Art pen
Waterproof black drawing ink

1 *The A4 rough sketch, drawn with black ballpoint pen on copy paper, incorporates all the main features of this view of the site. The artist creates a visual frame for the view by including overhanging trees at the top and sides of the image and planters at the bottom that link the outer edges of the rendering and provide an interesting contour.*

At the same time, the detail and balance of the composition is considered: the lamp standard and canopies located at the centre of the drawing will need some dark tonal values behind them so that they will stand out in the final image.

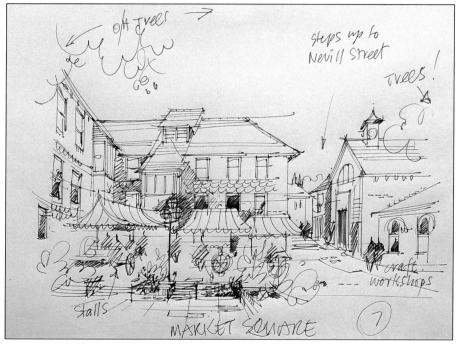

2 *Using a fine-nibbed art pen, the rough is copied onto heavy watercolour paper of a larger format proportional to the dimensions of the rough. The illustrator refers to the architect's plans and elevations as the drawing develops, but having worked out the composition in some detail in the rough stage, can give his main attention to the quality of the line work for the final version. The drawing is carefully structured, but follows the loose, lively style of the rough sketch.*

3 The first application of colour washes establishes the principal areas of the composition. Windows are brushed in with Winsor blue, darkened with indigo on the lower panes. A light wash of burnt sienna mixed with the blue is used to lay an overall tone for the brickwork. Indigo is spotted into the brown tones while they are still wet to strengthen the values behind the central detail. The same colour mix is applied to shadow areas in the foreground of the rendering.

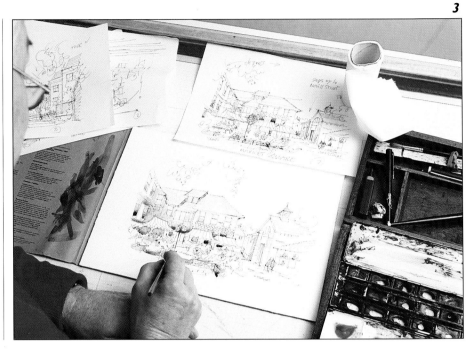

3

4

5

4 The grey-blue tones of the roofs are added in indigo mixed with cobalt blue, again using pure indigo to emphasize the darker tonal values. The greens used to brush in the general shapes of the foliage of trees and plants consist of a mixture of indigo and yellow ochre.

5 With the general pattern of the colour composition rapidly emerging, the hues are gradually enhanced by further washes to develop each area in more detail. The canopies are brushed with yellow ochre. A mix of yellow ochre and sap green is used to give a brighter tint to the foliage, and subtle touches of pure sap green, burnt sienna and indigo add depth and form. Contrasts of light and shade across the foreground and middle ground of the drawing are strengthened with further washes building the darker tones.

6

6 Additional colour contrast is added to the windows and canopies, using indigo and light red respectively. With the main colour areas described now in some detail, the sky colour can be brushed in. This illustrator prefers to colour the sky in the final stages of the rendering, although it is often common practice to do this first, to provide a basic colour key.

The sky is painted in five rapid steps: a slash of Winsor blue broadly brushed across the top; a pale mixture of yellow ochre and sepia washed in below, leaving bare paper between; below that, a wash of cobalt blue; a few strokes with a brush loaded with clean water, to blend the colour washes together; blotting of the colour to lift the tone and create an impression of pale clouds.

7

7 The overall tonal key of the painting is adjusted with heavy cast shadows laid into the foreground. Figures are also painted with dark tone, to give them a distinctive presence. Final emphasis is given to the window arches at right, using burnt sienna to strengthen the colour balance in this area of the rendering and link to the warmer colours on the left of the image.

8 On considering the completed illustration, the artist decides that the colour range across the centre of the image is too warm, and that one of the red and yellow canopies should be reworked in green and white, to create contrast in this focal area.

This is achieved by 'patching' the artwork: first it is laid on another piece of watercolour paper and the canopy shape is cut away through both thicknesses, using a sharp scalpel.

9

9 The plain paper cutout from the lower sheet is set into the artwork from the wrong side and taped across the back. This method of insertion leaves the patch flush with the original surface so that it is virtually invisible.

10 On the right side of the artwork, the patch is redrawn in the style of the other canopies and colour is added when the line work is dry.

11 The finished artwork shows how this late decision to alter the colour balance has given fresh focus through the contrast of the green and white canopy against the reds. It enhances the impression of detail in the busy area at the centre of the rendering.

Pencil and coloured pencil

Frank Costantino

This sequence shows, not the development of a single image, but the process of working toward the final rendering through a series of preparatory studies. In this case these procedures were unusually lengthy, because of the sensitivity of the project. A first-phase building completed by the developer had generated considerable reaction and controversy among local architects, city agencies and area civic groups. This forced the developer to change the architect and prepare a new design for a second tower, originally planned as an identical companion to the first. For the new project, both architect and developer required a precise, effective drawing that would placate detractors and help to reaffirm the developer's otherwise excellent reputation in the city.

From start to finish the process took six months, including meetings, reviews, delays and changes, and actual production. The principal's time on the final rendering was almost four weeks.

Architect Robert A.M. Stern
Rendering Assistants Arthur Dutton and Catherine Costantino

THE BRIEF

The perspective would serve several purposes, relating to the architect's design development phase, the developer's corporate review process, the city's planning approval requirements and promotional publicity directed to prospective tenants and the public in general.

The medium was determined by the architect and developer, who had seen examples of the drawing technique.

MATERIALS

Wax-based coloured pencils
Mechanical pencil and drafting leads
Graphite pencils, 5B to HB
Detail paper
Tracing paper
Drafting film

1 A site photograph of existing
conditions (left) provided by the client
forms the basis of a freehand sketch
overlay (right) showing the
approximate position of the new two-
building complex. The sketch is
developed from a pencil tracing of the
photographic view.

1

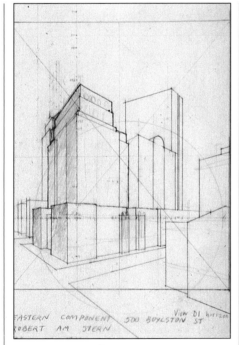

2

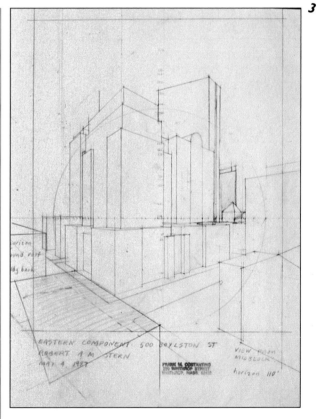

3

2 The photograph is subsequently
eliminated as the drawing base when
more accurate projections utilizing the
photographic viewpoint are found to
obstruct the view of the tower in the
left background. This plan-projected
view is the first of a view analysis
series eventually consisting of thirteen
different 'massing' perspectives. As
compared to the view derived from
the photograph, the station point is
slightly to the left and the horizon line
somewhat lower. The studies are
used to assess the overall composition
and an effective relation between all
volumes.

3 This study has a more distant
station point, further to the left than
that in the previous example, and a
higher horizon line. This results in an
unrelieved overlap of structures from
foreground to background that is
considered unsatisfactory.

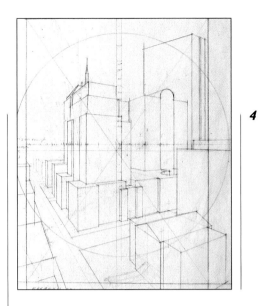

4 *This is the preferred perspective from the view analysis phase, incorporating all the major components in a visually descriptive manner, and almost all within the cone of vision. The building in the right foreground falls outside the cone of vision and is subject to distortion; it requires a secondary, adjusted projection to achieve its proper proportions.*

5

5 *A final line layout is developed, based on the selected study. The disadvantage of the layout being bisected by a slightly higher than mid-height horizon line through the corner building are to some degree offset by the spire of the background tower and the taller planar building on the right. The format is elongated by the inclusion of the existing buildings in the right foreground; a different crop might have produced a square, or even horizontal format.*

The relationship of the spired tower to the overlapping volume of the subject building is 'finessed' through four separate studies. In design changes to the building proposals, the height of the new tower block has been lowered; together with the discovery of more accurate reference drawings for the spired tower, this results in a more favourable relation between the existing and proposed structures in the final composition.

6 *The line perspective is drawn up with standard mechanical drafting leads, and coloured pencil detail is added that will provide clarity for transfer of the drawing in later stages.*

6

7

7 *On freehand sketch overlays of the line perspective, shade and shadow studies are devised to indicate a morning (left) and afternoon (right) sun angle. Given the north-westerly orientation of the principal facade of the new building, the shades and shadows of an afternoon sun are found to provide an effective pattern of light and dark, vertical and horizontal surfaces that enhances the composition.*

8

8 *Accurate shadow projections are drawn in red on a same-size photocopy of the line layout. Because of the complexity of the perspective, it is considered preferable to prepare this shadow study separately from the line drawing.*

9

10

9 *For the client's review and presentation needs, a full-size study of tonal values is drawn, using black wax-based pencil on a photocopy of the line layout. This sketchy monochrome model also provides valuable reference for the final drawing stages of the project.*

10 *A highly finished monochrome rendering is completed using a range of graphite pencils, from 5H for the sky to HB for the shadows. It is drawn on heavy translucent rag tracing paper (vellum), so the original line drawing can be used as an underlay, eliminating the need to transfer the drawing to the final support. Reference for the detailed development of the overall view is taken from the original photograph supplemented by occasional site visits.*

12 *The final stage of this long drawing process is a full-colour rendering, using wax-based coloured pencils applied to front and back of a photographic print on drafting film. The print is slightly under-exposed to allow for the added value range of the colours, and this reduction of tonal values also allows for a different configuration of sky and clouds to be superimposed. The translucency of the film provides a receptive base for mixing the pencil colours through the film, a process not unlike the layered application of watercolour washes, which results in a striking luminescent quality.*

Because substantial design changes were made to the subject building after completion of the monochrome rendering, a separate pencil drawing of the tower has been photographically composited into the print. This insertion is effectively camouflaged by deft handling of the colour work.

11

11 *This detail picture shows the high resolution of the pencil shading and the slight texture deriving from the 'tooth' of the paper surface. The characteristic qualities of the medium and support – the reflective greyness of the pencil leads and semi-opacity of the paper – create a bluish-grey image with a mid-range level of contrast. If required, photographic prints can be made on opaque paper in which the tonal range can be modified and contrasts enhanced.*

PORTFOLIO

AN INTERNATIONAL CATALOGUE OF ARCHITECTURAL RENDERINGS

Gilbert Gorski

Dain Bosworth Tower, Minneapolis, Minnesota, 1989
Architect: Lohan Associates
Coloured pencil
966×508mm (38×20in)

The illustrator was challenged by the client to present the proposed building in a highly dramatic setting, hence the night view lit by glowing surfaces and searchlight beams. The background buildings, although accurately portrayed, were moved in closer to intensify the sense of urban energy surrounding the site. The image was subsequently displayed on the construction site in a reproduction 7.6m (25ft) high.

Peter Roper

Tour McGill College, Montreal, 1990
Client: Groupe Everest
Coloured pencil on ozalid paper
508×763mm (20×30in)

The detailed volume of the building was created on a Macintosh computer using a 3-D imaging programme. The wireframe image was rotated to obtain the best rooftop view, which then formed the basis of a drawing locating the building within the context of the night-time landmarks of downtown Montreal.

Leonard Curtis

Swallow Place, Oxford Street, London, 1987
Architect: Rolfe Judd
Ink and watercolour
763×559mm (30×22in)

For this illustration forming part of a planning application, an important aspect of the brief was to lessen the impact of the building within the general context of the location by emphasizing the vitality at street level of this major thoroughfare.

Frank Costantino

Mount Sinai Hospital Renovation, New York City, 1990
Architect: Wank Adams Slavin Associates
Watercolour
394×534mm (15½×21in)

The basis of this illustration was a computer-generated layout of existing and proposed elevations of the facade, over which the artist projected the numerous design details and the context of adjacent buildings, landscaping, existing trees, and typically busy traffic. A limited palette was selected to achieve the warm brightness of spring daylight.

The light on the building being diffused due to its near-northerly orientation, the contrast provided by the darkly shadowed trees in the foreground enhances the luminescent effect.

Stewart White

Market Square, Pennsylvania Avenue, Washington DC, 1990
Client: Pennsylvania Avenue Development Corporation
Watercolour on board and Xerox transfer
763×1017mm (30×40in)

This aerial perspective is one of a series of renderings showing seven development projects on the Pennsylvania Avenue site. The original artwork is relatively large scale, although intended primarily for use in a brochure showing all of the proposed developments.

Tamotsu Yamamoto

Gleneagles, Lake Placid, New York, 1989
Architects: Todd Lee/Clark/Rozas Associates, Inc.
Watercolour
247×343mm (13½×21½in)

This rendering was executed as part of a proposal to the owner for renovation of and additions to an existing hotel facility. An important aspect of the presentation was to convey the beauty of the environment and landscaping on the site, as well as the character of the building.

Takashi Yanagisawa

Kobe Portpia Hotel, 1981
Client: Nikken Sekkei Ltd.
Airbrushed watercolour
540×540mm (21¼×21¼in)

Warm colours and an overall soft reflection create an effect of harmony between the hues of the building and the sky. The illustration is photorealist in its depiction of light on surfaces, and in its meticulous detail.

Orest Associates

Toronto Plaza, Toronto, 1984
Designer: Orest Associates
Tempera and gouache
1017×763mm (40×30in)

THE TORONTO PLAZA

This rendering illustrates a proposal for an office building with restaurant, private club and health club on the top two floors. The dark foreground tones and distant building silhouettes emphasize the main subject, using areas of flat colour characteristic of these paint media.

Tomoyuki Murayama

Kanematsu Building, 1990
Client: Shimizu Corporation
Gouache
210×297mm (8¼×11⅝in)

In illustrating the lobby area of this planned construction, rather than emphasize details, the artist has chosen to highlight the hard quality of materials in the interior, brilliantly capturing the qualities of transparency and reflectance to make an intriguing and dynamic composition.

Hoffpauir/Rosner Studio

50 Avenue Montaigne, Paris, 1990
Architect: Kohn Pedersen Fox Conway
Watercolour
407×407mm (16×16in)

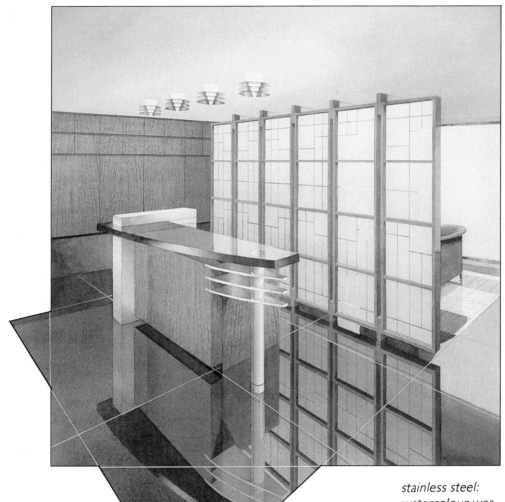

This drawing represents a typical reception area for the building. The initial perspective was produced on computer using architect's blueprints, and material samples were also supplied by the architect. The variety of materials included granite, wood and stainless steel: watercolour was chosen as the most appropriate medium for effective rendering of their surface qualities.

Michael McCann

Queens University Library, Ontario, 1990
Architect: Kuabara Payne McKenna Blumberg
Watercolour
305×508mm (12×20in)

The renderings for this competition entry, subsequently the winning design, for the Queens University Library were intended to convey the mood and lifestyle of the location as well as the image of a contemporary building developed in the Gothic tradition.

The serenity and atmosphere of this image represent the scenic character of the city of Ontario and evoke the fresh, optimistic mood of the illustrator's own experience of campus life.

David Eccles

Ludgate House, Bankside, London, 1985
Architect: Fitzroy Robinson partnership
Acrylic watercolour
712×483mm (28×19in)

The building's design was intended to be bright and extrovert, and one of the aims of the rendering was to point up the contrast with neighbouring structures.

Reflective cladding on the curved and angled facades affords a suggestion of other buildings outside the scope of the view, while the strong road and railway elements are intended to

emphasize the site's connection with the City of London across the river.

Gordon Grice

King Abdulaziz University, Jeddah, Saudi Arabia, 1990
Architects: Webb Zerafa Menkes Housden/Keith Loffler
Ink and coloured pencil
506×814mm (20×32in)

This aerial view of the proposed layout of the university was required to show both the scope of the project and the intricacy of the design. The problem of illustrating the extent of the site and the degree of detail was solved by using a fine technical pen to describe form, pattern and texture down to the small-scale detail, then working with coloured pencils on front and back of a reproduction on drafting film to develop the impression of the building materials and colourful planting scheme.

Thomas Norman Rajkovich

Ars Recte Aedificandi, Livorno, 1990
Architect: Thomas Norman Rajkovich
Watercolour and ink wash
508×610mm (20×24in)

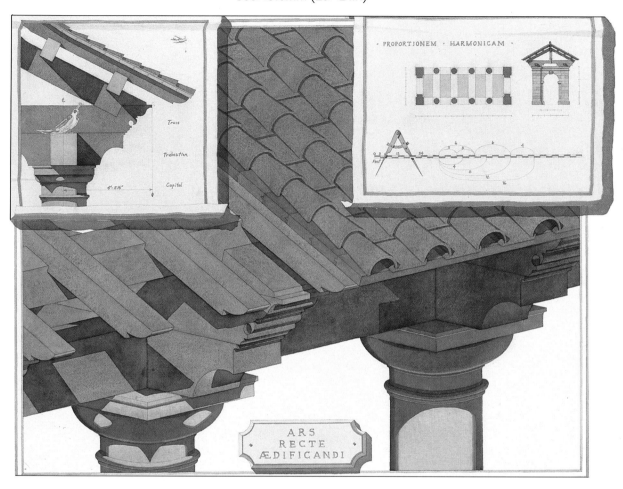

This design proposal for a new covered Tuscan market loggia for the piazza of a small Italian town is represented in the tradition of eighteenth century trompe l'oeil *painting. A diverse range of architectural information is synthesized into a single image, thematically composed to include elements of construction, detail and proportion. The title, meaning 'the art of proper building', reveals the important didactic aspect of the illustration.*

Suns Hung

Trinity Building, New York City, 1989
Architect: Swanke, Hayden, Connell Architects
Pen and ink with airbrushed colour
610×483mm (24×19in)

This rendering illustrates the proposed renovation of a classical building with intricate detail. Subdued treatment of the surrounding buildings and the dark tones of the sky accentuate the central subject. Strategic use of strong colour creates points of focus in an image mainly reliant on tonal values.

Thomas W. Schaller

First Citizen's Bank Building, Raleigh, North Carolina, 1990
Architect: Kohn Pedersen Fox
Watercolour
1017×763mm (40×30in)

FIRST CITIZENS BANK CENTER
RALEIGH, NORTH CAROLINA

The transparency of watercolour makes it arguably the most effective medium for conveying in two dimensions a sense of depth and the dramatic impact of light. In this image the light, coming from the actual white of the paper, was composed to emphasize most effectively the structure and character of the building.

Christopher Gibbs

Resort Project, Phuket, Thailand, 1990
Client: Projects International, Hawaii
Coloured pencil on photocopy enlargement of original
pencil drawing
165×330mm (6½×13in)

This drawing describes a project in the earliest stage of development. Information was taken from photographic sources, including the architectural and environmental factors pertinent to design considerations. The character of the site was also developed in conversations with the architects, 'scripting' the nature and sequence of events a visitor to the project might experience. In this way the renderings were integral to the design process, raising specific questions and enabling design solutions to be developed.

Stanley Doctor

Mahukona Cabanas, Kona Coast, Hawaii, 1990
Architect: Gage Davis
Coloured pencil and opaque watercolour
508×763mm (20×30in)

To create this image, hand-rendered detail was applied to a computer-generated base layout, from a purpose-designed software programme that enables a precise drawing to be plotted from the most basic design information. The artist's elaboration of the view aims to capture the spirit of the design and communicate a sense of place.

Eugene Radvenis

Arts Club Theatre, Vancouver, 1990
Architect: Bing Thom, Architects
Mixed media
407×508mm (16×20in)

This evening view depicts an opening night at the Arts Club Theatre, located on a prime corner in a popular night-life area of downtown Vancouver. The site is an ideal location for the mixed-use theatre, restaurant and shopping complex. The lacy framework and glowing transparency of the glass box-like structure allows the activity within to be displayed.

Robert McIlhargey

Esposicion Universal Sevilla 1992, 1988
Architect: Expo 92
Mixed media
992×992mm (39×39in)

This is part of a drawing programme commissioned for an exhibition that would explain to the public, participants and press the cultural and planning objectives of the 1992 World Fair in Seville. It is one of 40 renderings showing key site features and amenities. The mixed media technique consists of airbrushed colour on a black line print, with hand-coloured detail and texture developed in watercolour, marker, pencil and coloured pencil. Final highlights were applied in tempera using ruling pen, brush and airbrush.

169

Kazuko Shimada

Rushin Hotel Project, 1987
Client: Zou Sekkei Shudan
Pen and ink, silkscreen
728×1030mm (28½×40½in)

A sculpture rising from the land represents human activity in the primordial forest. The gradations of colour and texture possible with the silkscreen process suit the subject admirably and bring out its atmospheric quality rather than its precise design details.

Eiji Mitooka

Tomam Resort Project, 1990
Client: Alpha Corporation Co. Ltd.
Technical pen with Pantone overlay and airbrushing
940×760mm (37×30in)

The bird's eye view of the resort was designed as publicity material for use in newspapers and magazines. It was one part of a full perspective rendering, intended as an introduction to the natural surroundings and rich amenities available at the resort, to convey its scale and the recreational possibilities on offer.

T. Kelly Wilson

Canary Wharf, London, 1989
Architect: Koetter/Kim Architects
Graphite pencil on Strathmore paper
1071×381mm (40×15in)

Using classical conventions, this rendering provides a detailed tonal construction of the project, the subtleties of the drawing entirely achieved through careful shading and blending of H, 2H and 3H pencil leads. This time-consuming work was the third stage of this illustrator's process, the first being freehand sketch drawings determining the architectural subject and context within a compositional framework, the second stage a working up of the 'correct' perspective view, either freehand or by mechanical processing. Each stage is a reinterpretation, not a copy, of the previous visualization.

Doug Jamieson

International Arrivals Terminal, John F. Kennedy Airport, New York, 1990
Architect: Pei Cobb Freed & Partners
India ink wash and airbrushing
763×763mm (30×30in)

Orchestrating some dozen different light sources within the interior space was one of the challenging aspects of this rendering. Detail and texture are mainly subordinated to the diffuse glow emanating from the lantern crowning the central dome of the building. Monochrome rendering was considered an advantage, giving a certain abstraction to the image and achieving a dramatic quality that immediately engages the viewer. The soft surface qualities of ink wash and airbrushing lend elegance and subtlety to the range of tonal values

John Haycraft

National Maritime Museum, Sydney, 1987
Architect: Philip Cox Richardson Tayle & Partners
Tempera on artboard
762×1017mm (30×40in)

An aerial view was required to express the 'sail-shaped' roofs of the building, and was also helpful in giving depth to the wharf activities.

However, the architect wanted the rendering to look into the building and maintain a sense of human scale, so the artist has had to deal with the difficult proposition of a relatively low aerial viewpoint.

Peter Edgeley

South Bank development, Melbourne, 1989
Architect: Sprankle Lynd & Sprague/Buchan Laird & Bawden
Airbrushed acrylic and gouache
500×750mm (19½×29½in)

The proposed development is located in relation to known landmarks, such as the white steel tower in the middle-distance and the bridge in the foreground. The set-ups were based on site photographs, which accurately locate the towers within the scene.

The waterfront area was enhanced by increasing the depth of the river view and its reflections.

Edward Khong

Alexia bar and restaurant, Helsinki, 1989
Architect: Fitch-RS
Pencil, coloured pencil and pastel
594×841mm (23¼×33in)

This is a working sketch giving a first impression of the restaurant and bar area as customers would see it on arrival. The drawing was part of the architect's presentation to the client for approval of the scheme. The rendering was required to convey the atmosphere to be enjoyed by potential users and the warming glow of the finishes and lighting was an important consideration in the illustrator's brief.

Dan Harmon

Metro Center, Hartford, Connecticut, 1990
Architect: Thompson, Ventulett & Stainback
Watercolour
483×661mm (19×26in)

The rendering of the office tower lobby aims to include the maximum of available information within one view: the space of the lobby, the location of elevators, cross-axial connectors, and the variety of materials contributing to the character of the interior. The effect of strong sunlight within the space suggests the openness of the wall shown in foreshortened view at right.

Ronald Love

Hotel/Condominium, Vancouver, 1990
Architect: W.T. Leung
Pen and ink with acrylic
610×483mm (24×19in)

A literal interpretation of this project in its city context was needed to satisfy the requirements of city planners, developers and potential investors. To give mood and drama to the illustration, it was executed with a colour palette representing late afternoon light.

Robert Cook

Renaissance Center, Bridgeport, Connecticut, 1989
Architect: Architects Environmental Collaborative
Tempera
763×458mm (30×18in)

In a design competition to raise the 'After 5pm vitality' of a decaying downtown area of the city of Bridgeport, this rendering was chosen to become the focal point of the effort. The low-level evening sunlight throws the new development into sparkling relief, set against the shadowed background of the existing cityscape and the dark tones of the foreground landscaping.

Samuel Ringman

Goodman Residence, Houston, 1990
Architect: Elby S. Martin
Watercolour
330×660mm (13×26in)

The soft, atmospheric quality of watercolour was chosen to depict this large, elegant residence surrounded by pines. The romantic effect of misty morning light is achieved through the use of grey washes of varied strengths, with colour used primarily for focus.

Peter Huf

House in house, Brewster, Massachusetts, 1991
Architect: Anthony Tappe & Associates
Computer generated image

This combination image shows one of the advantages of computer work: different elements of the project once visualized can be duplicated, manipulated and overlaid, pasted into a composite picture. Here a model, section, floor plan and interior view constructed in Dynaperspective are given the focus of the human viewpoint by insertion of a figure scanned from a magazine picture.

Shu-Xiang Xi

Dana Farber Cancer Institute, Boston, Massachusetts, 1988
Architect: Shepley Bulfinch Richardson and Abbott, Inc.
Watercolour
610×914mm (24×36in)

This rendering illustrates new research laboratories built over an existing six-storey section of the Institute. The line and wash technique involves the use of sensitive pencil line, not ink drawing.

Colour work on the materials was kept subtle and light in value to make the building stand out from the darker background.

Gerald Green

Atlantic House, Holborn Viaduct, London, 1988
Architect: Rolfe Judd Group Practice
Watercolour and gouache
458×686mm (18×27in)

It was important in this illustration to portray clearly the full strength and clarity of the architectural statement being made, and this was achieved primarily by providing strong tonal counterchange.

Dark reflected images were introduced into the upper glazed areas from the white exposed steel framing.

This contrast was repeated at ground-floor level, giving additional emphasis to the lighter buff and blue stone features, set against darker recessed window spaces. Dark shadows and brightly coloured foreground vehicles further developed this theme.

The office of Zaha Hadid

Hamburg Hafenstrasse Project, 1989
Architect: The office of Zaha Hadid
Acrylic on paper mounted on linen
1000×1765m (39¼×69½in)

The painting is a composite of various studies of the corner building on Hamburg Hafenstrasse. The studies are a tool for refining the final design. Different perspective views were chosen to examine the building in the round.

Katsumi Yoshitani

Nippon Bank Osaka Branch, 1980
Client: Nikken Sekkei Ltd.
Watercolour
450×900mm (17½×35⅝in)

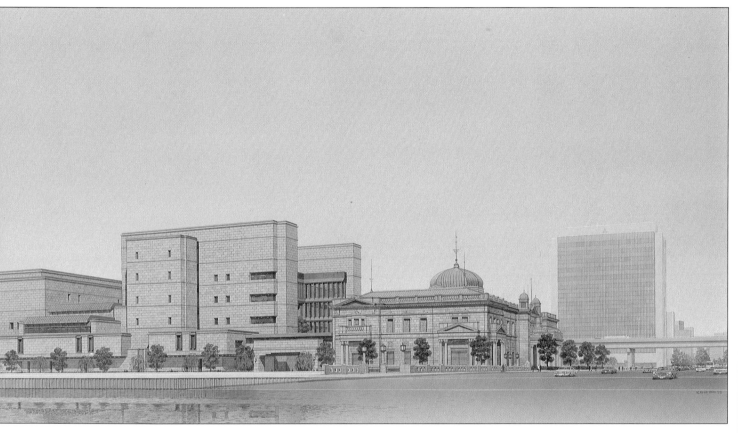

This advanced building is designed to blend with the surrounding scenery, including old structures along the front road. The perspective makes a point of this, toning down conspicuous elements and using greens and blues on the exterior walls and roof. Since much of the building is of granite construction, the rendering has been executed on grey paper, in pencil and watercolour. For the sky, opaque colours and a touch of airbrush work create the right effect.

Hisao Konishi

Osaka State House Proposal, 1989
Client: Nikken Sekkei Ltd, Osaka Technology Centre
Pencil, watercolour, airbrushing on photographic print
430×310mm (17×12¼in)

This interesting and very subtle use of mixed media portrays a vast structure as a backdrop for the ceremonial activity taking place within it. The building is rendered mono-chromatically, whereas the meticulous and very important details at ground level are picked out with spot colour.

Salvatore Grande

Yateen Centre, Manama, Bahrain, 1985
Architect: Felipe Yofre, Intec Bahrain
Silkscreen
430×660mm (17×26in)

This illustration was prepared for a commercial brochure. It is based on an ink line drawing, with use of screenprinting in four colours to produce the final rendering suitable for reproduction.

The synthesis of fine line work with the chromatic quality of the evenly toned colour passages results in an image of extreme clarity.

Mona Brown

New York City Coliseum, 1985
Architect: James Stewart Polshek & Partners
Coloured pencil on black museum board
623×534mm (24½×21in)

This rendering was a competition entry, the night view selected to create a dramatic impact. In order to obtain a high degree of credibility and accuracy, night-time site photography was employed for the artist's reference.

Paul Stevenson Oles

Pelli Canary Wharf Tower, London, 1988
Architect: Cesar Pelli
Wax-based pencil on white Strathmore board
508×381mm (20×15in)

This is a daytime view of the Canary Wharf Tower in London's docklands, using the devices of a low station point, a broad range of tonal gradation and reduction of distracting or extraneous elements to achieve a clear, dramatic view of the building. A night view was later executed, also designed to demonstrate the imposing presence of what was to be the tallest building in the UK.

Nobuo Kadowaki

Piramide, 1989
Architect: Kazumasa Yamashita
Mixed media
750×750mm (29½×29½in)

Both ground-level and aerial perspectives are incorporated into this work, to show the layout of the scheme in depth. This unusual combination of images makes a most effective composition in its own right.

John S. Robinson

Hotel Complex, Harare, 1991
Architect: Hok International Ltd
Watercolour and coloured pencil
548×610mm (18×24in)

In this illustration, considerable effort went into capturing the quality of the African sky and the planting surrounding the hotel. The upper levels of the building are painted against a strong blue section of the sky to accentuate the crispness of the architecture, while behind the lower levels the colour has been warmed to give a visual continuity between the building and its environment.

Octavio Balda

Treff Hotel, Hamburg, 1990
Architect: Raines Steffen
Wax-based coloured pencil and airbrushing
458×610mm (18×24in)

This illustration was intended for publication in a Swedish magazine, the original client for the project being based in Sweden, so the artist chose to convey the distinctive quality of natural light in Scandinavian countries. The light throws the architectural forms into sharp relief and intensifies the colours of the materials, against a background of brilliant blue sky.

Philip Crowe

Centre Gate, Leeds, 1990
Architect: Philip Lees Associates
Gouache and pastel dry wash
400×600mm (15¾×23½in)

This is one of two views of a low-rise city centre office complex to be sited in a harsh industrial landscape in process of regeneration: the rendering was to place emphasis on the proposed extensive planting around the building.

Dark tones in the foreground and the highly reflective surface qualities of the metal-clad roof and glazing ensure that the building has a firm base but appears as light in structure as possible.

Minoru Azuchi

JR Tokai Shinnano-machi Project, Tokyo, 1990
Client: Lynx/JR Higaninippon
Marker
728×1030mm (28½×40½in)

This perspective shows a typical big-city project in Tokyo, rendered in a style representing a futuristic, condensed image of the planned construction. The perspectivist was asked to create for the viewer the sensation of tumbling through the air, to which the rapidity of a free marker technique is ideally suited.

Michael Reardon

International Trade Mart, Osaka, 1990
Architect: Studios Architecture/Nikken Sekkei Ltd
Coloured pencil
763×458mm (30×18in)

The elevated viewpoint of this illustration dramatizes the height of the long, narrow space within the central atrium of the Trade Mart. The unusual impact of the image also derives from its scheme of strong, vivid colour.

Jan Matuszczak

Office building, Melbourne, 1988
Architect: Perrott Lyon & Mathieson
Transparent and opaque watercolour
590×840mm (23×33in)

*An aerial view
was chosen as
the best way to
describe the
building's
proximity to the
Exhibition
Gardens and
Melbourne's
central business
district.*

Noriya Matsumura

Kobe Port Island (first proposal), 1983
Client: Kobe City Municipal Department Bureau
Gouache, airbrushing and photomontage
400×500mm (15¾×19½in)

This is the planned reconstruction of Kobe Port Island. Twenty-seven buildings have already been planned for the site, and are included in the montage of perspectives and photographs. In between these buildings, other imaginary structures are shown – apartment blocks, fashion centres and kindergartens.

Rael Slutsky

Chicago Place, Chicago; 1986
Architects: Skidmore, Owings & Merrill and Solomon Cordwell Buenz & Associates, Inc.
Technical pen and ink on drafting film with coloured pencil and airbrushing on photo-mural paper
763×458mm (30×18in)

The project is a multi-use development including eight floors of retail space and three floors of offices, the remainder being apartments. The site is Chicago's prestigious and historic North Michigan Avenue where set-backs and height precedents must be respected. The challenge to the illustrator was to portray the activity in the retail areas at street level while strongly featuring the residential tower behind. Pen and ink provided high levels of definition of detail, with colour used for accent and focus.

Richard Baehr

Trump Palace, New York City, 1989
Architect: Frank Williams & Associates
Tempera on grey board
954×458mm (37½×18in)

A special point of the client brief for this illustration was to emphasize the height of the building, therefore the horizon line was kept low, but leaving enough depth to give a distinct view of the street plane. The gold top of the building is an important feature, here enhanced by the relatively dark tone of the sky.

Richard Sneary

Kansas City Museum Greenhouse, 1987
Architect: Solomon Claybaugh
Ink and watercolour
178×229mm (7×9in)

This is one of a series of seven illustrations, produced in small format to accommodate both its intended use in a brochure and cost considerations. An ink drawing was developed from an old and poor-quality monochrome photograph, and was then reproduced on watercolour paper and mounted on board. The main aim of the colour rendering was to achieve the qualities of light in the greenhouse structure – transparency, brightness and reflection – with sufficient intensity and contrast to compete with photographic images reproduced in the brochure.

Hajime Ono

Mizuno Karuzawa Tennis Club, 1981
Client: Zou Architect & Planning/Musashi Enterprise
Watercolour
500×707mm (19¾×27¾in)

This perspective shows a tennis club to be built in Japan's famous resort area of Karuzawa. The transparency of watercolour is used to good effect to give depth to the illustration, particularly in the distant treescape.

Richard Rees

Hong Kong Air Cargo Transport Ltd Building, Hong Kong Airport, 1989
Architect: Llewelyn-Davies Weeks (Hong Kong)
Airbrushed watercolour and ink
407×610mm (16×24in)

This was one of a pair of renderings taken from opposite sides of this unusual building, in which floor-to-ceiling heights are much greater than normal to allow trucks onto every floor. The seven floors are equivalent in height to a twelve-storey building, so establishing the scale with sufficient context was very important. Sharp airbrush work emphasizes the building's clear geometry in the sub-tropical light.

Itsuo Kaiho

Tokyo traffic, 1988
Client: MHS Architects Planners & Engineers/Mr Hideaki Kubo
Watercolour, gouache and coloured ink
594×841mm (23¼×33in)

This project was designed for a site in what was once the heart of downtown Tokyo, recently neglected in favour of more fashionable places. It seeks to evoke the scale and mystery of traditional Japanese culture.

The building breaks down into comprehensible units, inviting to the passerby, rather than presenting the kind of monolithic blank facade typical of much modern development.

David Purser

59 Mansell Street, London, 1991
Architect: Roy Properties
Ink line and watercolour
458×305mm (18×12in)

The delicate handling of the medium is ideally suited to the simplicity of the subject, a modest office development in a busy city street. It brings out the detail of the mouldings, balustrades and carefully drawn figures. The false shadows in the foreground provide a solid base for the illustration.

William G. Hook

The Tower Building, Washington, 1990
Architect: NBBJ (renovation and remodelling)
Ink wash
458×229mm (18×9in)

This drawing shows not a proposed new building, but the effect of new ornamentation integrated with existing terracotta details on the facade. The sculptural qualities and inset window areas provided a good opportunity to experiment with tonal values in ink wash.

Elizabeth Day

Sandoz Laboratories, 1988
Architect: Ewing Cole Cherry Parksy
Watercolour
305×458mm (12×18in) (detail)

An aerial view of the project was selected to show the volumes of the proposed laboratory and the layout of an interior courtyard. The warm tones of the building itself are complemented in the rendering by autumnal colouring in the landscaping of the site.

GMW Partnership

Office development, 54 Lombard Street, London, 1991
Architect: GMW Partnership, Architects
Computer-generated image

This is an external lighting design study of a full-scale 3-D building model created and rendered with Sonata software running on a Silicon Graphics Workstation. The combination of subtleties of lighting and complexity of building forms shows state-of-the-art computer graphics at its most impressive.

Fumiaki Fukunaga

Hokkai Can Company Ltd, Nasu Resort House, 1990
Client: Obayashi Corporation
Acrylic
430×600mm (17×23½in)

The location of this project is the Nasu Highlands, a treasure trove of plant life with abundant trees, shrubs and flowering plants and spectacular scenic views. The landscape setting was an important feature of the rendering, which would be carried in the company brochure, as the client hoped it would offer a particular aesthetic attraction to young people.

Katsuhiko Nakamura

The Kokeshi-kan diagram, 1982
Client: Kuroishi-shi, Aomori Prefecture
Watercolour
830×630mm (32½×24¾in)

This rendering shows a proposed studio for manufacture of kokeshi dolls. The combination of plan, elevation and perspective not only makes an attractive composition but gives the maximum amount of information about the proposals. The low viewpoint emphasizes the landscape interest of the surroundings.

Richard Rochon

Duke University Law School, Durham, North Carolina, 1990
Architect: Gunnar Birkett & Associates, Inc.
Airbrushing and wax-based coloured pencil
559×804mm (22×34in)

Working on both sides of high-translucency drafting film enables the illustrator to increase the range of subtleties in hues and tonal values and also enhances the transparency of the wax-based coloured pencils.

The composition is designed to give the most complimentary view of the subject, with site photographs used to provide realistic context.

Peter Wels

Kunsthalle, Hamburg
Architect: Prof. O.M. Ungers
Wax-based coloured pencil
763×1220mm (30×48in)

The proposed 'art island' museum building in Hamburg is shown here in its municipal context. The project is devised as an extension to the chain of older museum buildings already in existence. This rendering was first developed on computer and then examined from several possible viewpoints.

Supplementary reference was provided in site photographs taken from the selected viewpoint. The colour balance of the image is intended to direct the viewer's eye to the project itself and its immediate surroundings.

Wilbur Pearson

Spinnaker Pointe entrance, Miami, 1990
Architect: Robert West
Pencil on tracing paper (vellum)
458×610mm (18×24in)

The aim of this drawing, generated from architectural and landscape plans for the site, was a realistic depiction of the project entrance as it would appear with the landscape fully settled and matured after some years. This required extensive research into the plant species, their ultimate sizes and shapes. Field trips were undertaken to locate good examples to work from.

Thomas Spain

Windsor House, Vero Beach, Florida, 1990
Architect: Thomas Spain & Rolando L. Tanes
Pencil on tracing paper
254×483mm (10×19in)

This is one of two drawings that began as design sketches and evolved, through a process of making overlays, into full renderings of the design intentions of the project.

Soft pencil and tracing paper provided a responsive medium permitting both minor modifications and major revisions to the rendering.

Vic Carless

Power Tower 2, London, 1990
Architect: Paul Carless: Architects
Gouache
508×381mm (20×15in)

The architect wanted to convey the overall idea of the scheme, showing the planting integrated with the vertical steel and glass structure. At this initial stage, the overriding factor in the illustrator's brief was to express the excitement of the project.

Monkgol Tansantisuk

Capitol City Tower, Columbus, Ohio, 1990
Architect: The Stubbins Association
Wax-based coloured pencil on tracing paper (vellum)

Computer visualization was used in the early stages of this rendering to set up perspective line constructions of various views. A black and white drawing was made for presentation during design development. This colour rendering, used primarily for publication and promotional purposes, was required to provide high resolution and greater detail.

Joseph Henton

Development for GEC Plessey, UK, 1990
Architect: Alan Johnson Associates
Watercolour and gouache
534×610mm (21×24in)

This type and style of illustration conveys impact by means of form, volume and tonal values. The darker shades are those of the glazed elements, contrasting with the much lighter tones of the stone cladding, both set against a strong sky.

Philippe Martyniak

Johns Hopkins Plaza, Baltimore, 1990
Architect: Payette Associates
Pastel and coloured pencil
763×1017mm (30×40in)

This landscape rendering incorporates a famous feature of the locale, the Johns Hopkins dome, which is set against the background of a dramatically realized cloudy but bright sky.

The rendering is the last of more than 30 commissioned works for the same client over a three-year period, creating the challenge for the illustrator to maintain a fresh eye throughout the series of works.

Jonathan Adams

Hôtel du Département, Marseille, 1991
Architect: Alsop & Lyall
Graphite on tracing paper
594×420mm (23¼×16½in)

A building in which the exterior surface is predominantly glass picks up reflections by day and loses transparency, so for this rendering a night view was chosen to show the building lit from within to reveal its layering. The viewpoint representing approach by helicopter allows the complex roofscape to be seen and makes an acute angle to the facade, which yields reflected highlights. The drawing technique relies upon the removal of tone, after the graphite has been sprayed with fixative, primarily using a razor to scratch back the surface.

Dario Tainer and Kurt Williams

The Sporting Club Rooftop Terrace, Chicago, 1990
Client: The Sporting Club
Mixed media
763×763mm (30×30in)

The softness of paint and marker surface qualities contrasts with the hard, technical accuracy of the edges rendered with an airbrush. The technique helps to reinforce the different but related aspects of man-made and natural forms.

The purpose of the drawing was a funding application for purchase of trees to be situated in the rooftop garden.

Danny Meyer

Office development, London, 1990
Architect: Comprehensive Design Group
Watercolour and inks
420×594mm (16½×23¼in)

The illustrator's brief was to indicate the setting of the building in its context and emphasize the contrast of materials used, with particular attention to the reflection of the external grid in the mirror glass.

Wesley W. Richards

210 Euston Road, London, 1989
Architect: EPR Architects Ltd
Gouache
420×458mm (16½×18in)

This rendering of a new office building on one of the main thoroughfares of London illustrates its context in the existing streetscape, and its high-quality finishes. The surface qualities were achieved by using gouache either as body colour or as wash, depending upon the effect required.

INDEX

Page numbers in *italics* refer to illustration captions

A

accuracy 31
acrylics *55,* 67-9, *68, 69*
  acrylizing medium with gouache 64
  airbrushing 78, 79
  markers 74
Adams, Jonathan 218
'aerial perspective' 35-6, 46, 73
aerial viewpoints 22-3, *22,* 26-8, *27, 28*
aerosol sprays 80, *80*
airbrushing *17,* 33, 40, 41, 43, 53, *53, 55,* 63, 77-80, *77, 78, 79*
  step-by-step guides 92-5, 117, 118-23, 127-8, 131, 133
'artist's licence' 14-15
assimilation, colour 36-7, *36*
atmosphere, rendering 34, *35,* 42, 86, *114*
audio-visual presentations 16
automobiles *see* cars
axonometric constructions 23
Azuchi, Minoru 194

B

Baehr, Richard 199
Balda, Octavio 124-9, 192
ballpoint pens 50
bleeding off for impact 42, *42*
blending 47
  coloured pencil, 59, 60
  oil pastels 63
briefing *see* clients, interaction with
broad-line markers 52
broken washes 72
Brown, Mona 188
brushes:
  acrylics 68
  with gouache 64
  ink line 49
bubble-jet copiers 16

C

carbon pencils 47-8, *47*
Carless, Vic 214
cars, representing *40, 91, 99, 104, 127, 128, 135*

charcoal 41, 43, 47, *47,* 53
clients, interaction with 12-15, 18-20, 23, 24, 30, 31, 142
  impact of colour 54-5
climate and landscape 34-5, *70*
cloud effects *see* skyscapes
Coe, Don 136-41
collage 41, 81
coloured pencils *see* pencils
colours:
  light and 35-7, *36*
  media 52, 54-60
commissions *see* clients, interaction with
competitions 54
composition, general principles of 20-1
computers 16, 29-30, 82-3, *82, 83,* 97, *125*
concept sketches 10, 12, 18, *18*
Conté crayons 48, 63
Cook, Robert 179
copyscanners 39, 42, *42*
corrections:
  charcoal 47
  coloured pencils 57, 58
  display board 41
  gouache 55, 65
  graphite pencils 46
  markers 52, 55, 76
  pastels 61
  'patching' *140-1*
  pens 49, 50
  tempera 55, 67, *67*
  watercolours 55
  see also scratching out
Costantino, Frank 142-7, 153
costing commissions 18
cross-hatching *see* hatching
Crowe, Philip 193
Curtis, Leonard 152
curved horizontals *27*
cutaway views 33, *33*

D

Day, Elizabeth 206
Deputy, John 106-11
design input, unpaid 19
design sketches 10, *10,* 12, 18, *18, 46, 75*
designers' colours *see* gouache
diffuser sprays 80
dip pens *43,* 48-9, *48, 49*
display board 41
distortion in perspective 24-8, *24, 25, 26, 27*
Doctor, Stanley 167

dotting 44, *44,* 49, *51,* 59, 69, 72
  pastels 62
drafting film 42, 53, 58, 106, *107-11*
dry washes *52,* 53, *63*
  pastel with markers 76
  powdered pastel 62
dry-transfer tone 53
drybrush techniques 66, *66, 69, 69,* 72, *88, 134*
drying 56-7, *104*

E

Eccles, David 161
Edgeley, Peter 175
electronic scanners 39, 42, *42*
erasure *see* corrections
esquisses *see* design sketches

F

facade models 28-9
figures (people) 14, *14, 15,* 21, 33, 38, *99, 117, 135, 139*
fine-line markers 50-2, *51*
fixatives 45, 55, 57, 60, *99*
  markers *76*
  pastels 62
foliage *see* trees
format, illustration 42, *42*
fountain pens 52
frottage 45
Fukunaga, Fumiaki 208
furnishings 32-3, *33, 116-17*

G

gel medium for acrylics 68
Gibbs, Christoper 166
glass, representing *12,* 40
  gouache 92, *94, 131*
  pencil *98, 109, 111, 119, 125, 126, 127, 128*
  tempera *88, 91*
  watercolour *102, 117,* 118, *123, 139*
GMW Partnership 207
Gorski, Gilbert 150
gouache 55, 56, 57, 63-6, *64, 65,* 78, 79
  step-by-step guide 92-5, 130-5
  see also mixed media
Grande, Salvatore 187
graphite:
  pencils 45-7, *45, 46,* 96, *113, 125-6*

powdered *52, 101*
grass, representing *65, 90, 108-9, 110, 111, 133*
Green, Gerald 183
Grice, Gordon 162
grids, perspective 28
ground-level viewpoints 23
gum arabic 65, 71

H

Hadid, Zaha, office of 184
Harmon, Dan 177
hatching 44, *44,* 49, *49,* 51, *51,* 69
  cross-hatching 59, 62, 67
Haycraft, John 86-91, 96-9, 174
Henton, Joseph 216
highlighting 45, 62, 72-3, *74,* 76, 79, *89, 90, 91,* 92, *95, 134*
Hoffpauir/Rosner Studio 159
Hook, William G. 205
Huf, Peter 181
human interest *see* figures
Hung, Suns 118-23, 164

I

illustration board 42, 49, *74*
imaginative studies 17, *17,* 82, *82*
impasto *42,* 61, *91*
inks 49, *57*
  airbrushing 78
  line with markers 76
  line with watercolour 73, *73,* 118-23, 136-41
  washes 53
  see also mixed media
interiors 23, 32-3, *32, 33, 45, 58, 69,* 112-17
  airbrushing 78, *79*

J

Jamieson, Doug 173
jointed materials, colour and 36-7, *36*

K

Kadowaki, Nobuo 190
Kaiho, Itsuo 203
Khong, Edward 176
Konishi, Hisao 186

L

landscapes *12, 18, 20, 34-8,
  34, 37, 55, 59,* 61
    aerosol sprays 80
    panoramas *13, 22, 73*
    watercolour *70, 71*
laser copiers 16
layering 59, *60,* 62
light and colour 35-8
line techniques 40, 43
    markers 50-2, *51,* 74, 76
    see also pencils; pens
local colour 36-7
Love, Ronald 178

M

McCann, Michael 160
McIlhargey, Robert 169
markers *18,* 40, 50-2, 74-6,
  74, 75, 76
    spray markers 80
Martyniak, Philippe 217
masking 41, 46, 53, 55-6, *56,*
  108, 126, 127, 133
    acrylics 69
    airbrushing 78-9, *78, 121-2*
    gouache 66, *93-5*
    markers 75
    pastels 62, *62*
    watercolour 73
Matsumura, Noriya 197
matt medium for acrylics 68
Matuszczak, Jan 196
mechanical tones 53
Meyer, Danny 220
migration of pigments
  (gouache) 65
Mitooka, Eiji 171
mixed media 40-1, *41,* 66, *66,*
  80-1, *80, 81*
models 28-9
Monk, Tim 92-5
monochrome media 43-53
mood, rendering 34, *35,* 42,
  86, *114*
multiple-point perspectives
  25-6, *25*
Murayama, Tomoyuki 158

N

Nakamura, Katsuhiko 209
nibs 49, 50
night scenes *12, 48, 55*

O

oil paints 41
oil pastels 63, *63*
Oles, Paul Stevenson 124, 189
one-point perspectives *see*
  single-point perspectives
Ono, Hajime 201
'optical mixing' 59
Orest Associates 157
overhead projection 15-16, 39

P

panoramas *13, 22, 73*
papers *see* supports
pastels 40, 41, 56, 57, *60,*
  61-3, *61, 62, 63, 91*
    dry washes with markers 76
    see also mixed media
'patching' artwork *140-1*
Pearson, Wilbur 212
pencils *20, 35,* 45-8, *45, 46,*
  47, 54, 56, 57-60, *57, 58*
    pastel 61
    step-by-step guides 96-9,
      106-11, 124-9, 142-7
    with watercolour 70, *72,*
      73
    see also line techniques;
      mixed media
pens:
    dip *43,* 48-9, *48, 49*
    fountain 52
    marker 74-6, *74, 75, 76,* 80
    technical *43,* 50, *50*
    see also line techniques;
      mixed media
people *see* figures
permanence of artwork 55
perspectives 24-30, 32
photocopiers 16, 39
photographic paper, working
  with *79,* 81, *127-9, 143, 147*
photomontage *11,* 30-1, *30,*
  31, 63, *64,* 81
'pick-up' problems 64, 65,
  67, 74
plants, representing *see*
  grass; trees
powdered graphite *52*
pre-printed papers 81
presentation 15-16, *146*
press releases 18
project designers 12-15
Purser, David 100-5, 204

R

Radvenis, Eugene 168
Rajkovich, Thomas Norman
  163
Reardon, Michael 195
record-keeping 16, 38-9
Rees, Richard 202
reference sources 38-9, *39,*
  86, *114*
reproduction of artwork 42,
  53, 70
retarders for acrylics, 67, 68
retouching 63
Richards, Wesley W. 221
Ringman, Samuel 180
Robinson, John S. 191
Rochon, Richard 210
Roe, Harold R. 130-5
Roper, Peter 151

S

sanguine pencils 48
Schaller, Thomas W. 165
scraperboard 52-3, *52*
scratching out 41-2, 45, *63*
    see also corrections
sgraffito 59-60
Shimada, Kazuko 170
single-point perspectives
  24-5, *25,* 32
sketches *see* design sketches
skyscapes *21,* 34-5, 78-9, 80,
  81, 86
    gouache *22,* 66, *131*
    pastel 61
    pencil *97, 110, 127-8*
    watercolour *71,* 72, *102,*
      122, 139
Slutsky, Rael 198
Sneary, Richard 200
Spain, Thomas 213
spattering 66, 69, 72, 79
spray painting 40, 41, 43, 53,
  53, 63, 66, 76, 77-80, *77,*
  78, 79
stippling 49, 50, *51,* 66, 69,
  72
subterranean viewpoints 23,
  23
sunlight 34, 35-8
supports 41-2
    acrylics 68
    charcoal 47
    coloured pencils 58
    gouache/tempera 64-5, 67
    markers 51-2, 74-5, *74,* 76
    mixed media 81
    pastels 61-2, 63
    pen 50
    watercolours 70-1, *70,* 73
symmetrical divisions,
    problems of 20-1, *21*

T

Tainer, Dario, and Kurt
  Williams 219
talcum powder with markers
  76
Tansantisuk, Monkgol 215
technical pens *43,* 50, *50, 51*
tempera 55, 67, *67*
    step-by-step guide 86-91
texture paste with acrylics
  69
theoretical studies 17, *17,* 82,
  82
tonal rendering 43-4, *43,* 53,
  80
    charcoal 47, *47*
    markers 75-6
    pencils 58-9
tracing paper 42, 58
transfer tone papers 44
trees, representing *24,* 37-8,
  38, 72
    acrylics *69*
    gouache 66, *131, 134*
    pen *137*

pencil *97, 98, 108-9, 110,*
  126-7, 128
tempera *90, 91*
watercolour *104, 105, 122,*
  138

V

'value delineation system'
  (Oles) 124
vegetation, representing *see*
  grass; trees
vertical recession 25-6, *26*
video camera exploration of
  image 16
viewpoints 22-3
    identifying 19-20
visualization 10, 12, 17, 74,
  142
visualizers 39

W

'walk-through' simulation 16,
  136
water, representing 36-7, *36,*
  66, *66, 90, 107*
watercolours *19, 20, 34, 35,*
  40, 41, 43, 53, 70-3, *70, 71,*
  72, 73
    airbrushing 78, 79, *79, 81,*
      118-23
    correction 55
    diffuser sprays 80
    step-by-step guides 100-5,
      112-17, 118-23, 136-41
wax resist 44-5, 72, *105*
Wearne, Mark 112-17
Wels, Peter 211
wet-in-wet techniques 65, 68,
  71, *71,* 86
wetting agents with acrylics
  68
White, Stewart 154
white pencils 48, *48,* 60
Williams, Kurt (*and* Dario
  Tainer) 219
Wilson, T. Kelly 172
windows, *see* glass,
  representing

X

Xi, Shu-Xiang 182

Y

Yamamoto, Tamotsu 155
Yanagisawa, Takashi 156
Yoshitani, Katsumi 185

CREDITS

Opposite title page Thomas Norman Rajkovich; **contents page** John Deputy with Frank Costantino; **10** Spencer Fung; **11** Peter Edgeley; **12** (*top*) Philip Crowe; (*bottom*) Tomoyuki Murayama; **13** (*top*) Carlos Diniz Associates; (*bottom*) Vic Carless; **14** (*top*) Sauerbruch & Hutton; (*bottom*) Philip Crowe; **15** Philip Crowe; **16** Richard Rochon; **17** (*left*) Thomas Schaller; (*right*) Brendan Neiland; **18** (*top and bottom*) Philip Crowe; **19** Vic Carless; **20** (*top*) Peter Wels; (*bottom*) David Purser; **21** (*top*) Takuji Kariya; **22** (*top*) Philip Crowe; (*bottom*) Stewart White; **23** Stirling Wilford; **24** R. J. Henton; **25** Peter Edgeley; **26** (*top and bottom*), **27** Philip Crowe; **28** Tim Monk; **29** D.E.W.J.O.C.; **30** (*top*) Jim Kershaw; (*bottom*) Philip Crowe; **31** (*top and bottom*) Philip Crowe; **32** (*top*) Philippe Martyniak; (*bottom*) Robert Cook; **33** (*top*) Ambler & Haycraft; (*bottom*) Mark Wearne; **34** Robert Comazzi; **35** (*top*) Vic Carless; (*bottom*) Peter Roper; **36** (*top*) R.J. Henton; (*bottom*) Philip Crowe; **37** (*top*) Jan Matuszczak; (*bottom*) Philip Crowe; **38** (*top*) Danny Meyer; (*bottom*) Frank Costantino; **40** David Purser; **41** Robert McIlhargey; **42** Peter Edgeley; **43** Philip Crowe; **44** (*top*) Robert Gill; (*bottom*) Philip Crowe; **45** (*top*) Octavio Balda; (*bottom*) Thomas Spain; **46, 47,** Philip Crowe; **48** (*top*) Paul Stevenson Oles; (*bottom*) Philip Crowe; **49** Philip Crowe; **50** David Purser; **51** (*top*) Philip Crowe; (*bottom*) Michael Elavsky; **52** (*bottom*) Philip Crowe; **53** Suns Hung; **54** (*top*) Orest Associates; (*bottom*) Philip Crowe; **55** Lee Dunette; **57** (*top*) Nobuo Kadowaki; (*bottom*) Jan Matuszczak; **58** Philip Billingham; **59** (*top*) Richard Rees; (*bottom*) Philip Crowe; **60** Gordon Cullen; **61, 62, 63** Idris Walters; **64** (*top*) Richard Baehr; (*bottom*) Philip Crowe; **65** (*top*) Hisao Konishi; (*bottom*) Philip Crowe; **66** (*top*) Itsuo Kaiho; (*bottom*) Philip Crowe; **67** Ambler & Haycraft; **68** (*top*) Ronald Love; (*bottom*) David Eccles; **69** (*top*) Kenneth Bear; (*bottom*) David Eccles; **70** (*top*) Vic Carless; (*bottom*) Gerald Green; **71** (*top*) Leonard Curtis; (*bottom*) Wesley Richards; **72** (*top*) Takashi Yanagisawa; (*bottom*) Katsuhiko Nakamura; **73** (*top*) Richard Sneary; (*bottom*) Noriya Matsumura; **74** (*top*) Minoru Azuchi; (*bottom*) Philip Crowe; **75** (*top*) Michael Elavsky; (*bottom*) Salvatore Grande; **76** Philip Crowe; **77** John McCoy; **78** (*top*) Terry Niven; (*bottom*) John McCoy; **79** (*top*) Terry Niven; (*bottom*) John McCoy; **80** (*top*) Philip Crowe; (*bottom*) Eiji Mitooka; **81** (*top*) Salvatore Grande; (*bottom*) Eugene Radvenis; **82** (*top*) Chris Wilkinson/Random Access Architects; (*bottom*) Ali Sanei/Random Access Architects; **83** (*top*) G.M.W. Partnership; (*centre and bottom*) Guiliano Zampi.
The diagrams on pages 21, 24, 25, 27, 28 and 32 were drawn by Simon Roulstone.

Quarto would like to thank all of the architectural illustrators who have contributed work for reproduction in this book. Special thanks to Frank Costantino and to Rico Komanoya of Graphic Sha for their work in coordinating contributions from the USA and Japan respectively.